AF508423

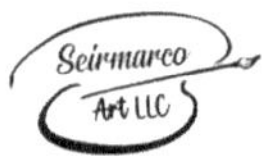

Seirmarco Art LLC
Reston, VA 20190

ISBN:

eBook	979-8-9891067-0-7
Paperback	979-8-9891067-1-4
Hardcover	979-8-9891067-2-1

Library of Congress Control Number: 2023922203

First Edition
Book Production and Publishing by Brands Through Books
brandsthroughbooks.com

www.peopleneedart.com

ART

YOU BE
THE JUDGE

Reawaken Your Instincts and Enjoy Art on Your Own Terms

LOUISE SEIRMARCO-YALE

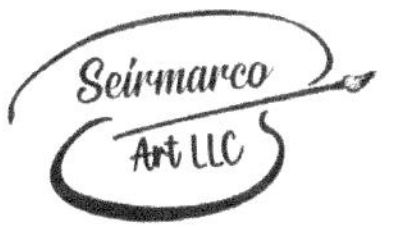

As close friends of Louise Seirmarco for fifteen years, we are thrilled to endorse her book, *Art, You Be the Judge: Reawaken Your Instincts and Enjoy Art on Your Own Terms*. Louise's authority as an author, teacher, and influencer in the visual arts shines through every page of this remarkable work. Her book is a beacon of hope for all who have ever felt intimidated by the world of art, assuring us that it is a world open to each and every one of us.
We wholeheartedly endorse *Art, You Be the Judge* and encourage anyone seeking to rekindle their love for art to embark on this empowering journey with Louise as your guide.

ANGELA INZERILLO and JAMES LAWSON,
Impact Biz LLC, Fairfax, VA

My friend & mentor & power partner.
Louise Seirmarco-Yale
is a leader,
is a treasure,
is a talent,
is a sage.
I've been in awe of this amazing human being since meeting her in 2004. In a room of thousands of beautiful people, she stood head and shoulders above the crowd quietly, humbly, and playfully.
There's an artist in each of us. To heal, to love, to be, to enjoy . . . these are all embedded in the pursuit of our inner artist. Thank you, Louise, for reminding and guiding us.

MARY GLYNN FISHER, Virginia Beach, VA

Louise Seirmarco-Yale has been devoted throughout her life to sharing her love of art with people. She is magnetic and enthusiastic when talking about art in museums or when making her own artwork available to others. I have known her since she worked in museum education at the Toledo Museum of Art where she espoused giving people the critical tools they needed to explore and validate their own impressions of the art they were seeing. This book is the fruition of her journey with art, one that she now shares to enable so many to explore their creativity with confidence.

JOAN ELISABETH REID, Baltimore, MD

I am a Steinway Artist and have the luxury of owning several of Louise's beautiful paintings and two stunning murals she created on my Hubbard harpsichord. These works of art are in my studio and greatly enhance my work as a performing artist. It is amazing how the two genres of art and music have influence over each other and work together. I am inspired by not only the colors in Louise's artwork, but the fluidity and blend of symmetry in her style. This is directly parallel to my work as a pianist and constantly inspires me to look beyond the printed music itself. It inspires me to be more creative in my own interpretations, to incorporate the flow of colors into the sound, and allow the symmetry in her artwork to become part of the rhythmic thread in music.

I commissioned Louise to create a mural on the lid and soundboard of my Hubbard harpsichord. This was a unique collaboration, during which I requested her to depict Mt. Vernon, Washington's home, on the lid, a favorite place of mine to visit. What she created is a masterpiece. The soundboard shows a collection of flowers and is strikingly personal. It is an absolute joy to play and own this beautiful harpsichord. Thank you, Louise, for adding this incredible dimension to my life, both personal and professional.

LISA EMENHEISER, Steinway Artist, Sterling, VA

Our friend's and family's conversations revolve around Louise's breathtaking creation. After two years of searching, with no success, for the perfect art decor for our custom-built home, Louise came to our rescue. Within one visit she listened to our vision and painted the most spectacular 6ft x 9ft masterpiece for our great room. The movement of water, sky and cliffs in the art piece draws you in to discover other aspects of the painting that are not obvious at first; the colors blend perfectly throughout the house.

CHRIS and KEN ROEBUCK, FL

I met Louise over twenty years ago through our children and quickly found out through conversation that she was an artist. Being a lover of art, I was intrigued, and wanted to see her work. When I went to her studio, my mind was blown! I loved her use of color, texture, multimedia, and her semi-representational approach to landscape and nature. I immediately felt drawn in to the strong yet subtle lines and colors of her work. In fact, one of her large pieces graces my living room wall, and everyone who visits remarks what a beautiful piece it is. It really is! I'm so happy to be able to start every morning with my coffee not only getting lost in the color and stories that this painting tells me but also being reminded on a daily basis what a beautiful spirit Louise is. She paints from her heart and soul. There is no doubt.

DALE REPSHAS, Reston, VA

Table of Contents

I want to dedicate this book to my family. In this book, you will learn how I have lived my truth, that family is everything.

I dedicate this book to my father, who always thought I was an artist and told me so. To my mother, who gave me the freedom to be as creative as I wanted without limits. To my loving sister Henrietta, who guided me to successful ways to achieve my dreams. To my brother, Joe, for passing along his extreme optimism to me—the component piece of "Dreaming Big." And to my sister Lynn for her consistent belief in my ability to do anything—what a gift.

My family support, of course, includes my wonderful, supportive husband, Wendel Yale, whose steadfast faith in me has never wavered. He has always encouraged me to be "me." His support was universal and present in every area of my life. He let me pursue my own path to fulfillment of my potential wherever it led and however it affected our married life. Another extremely positive influence in my life.

To my son, Derek, who has been the greatest gift of my life. He opened my heart's capacity to love and be loved from the moment he arrived. He brought me Lauren, whose loving support fit right in with our family values of love through freedom.

In writing this, I am even more aware of how lucky I have been to be surrounded by those who sought to protect my talents. These wonderful people allowed me to retain the confidence of a child to think I could do or be anything I wanted. I did just that because of them. If you believe it, you can achieve it.

Introduction

WHY HAVE I WRITTEN THIS BOOK? I HAVE FOUND THAT MANY ADULTS feel that they do not know anything about art and that art is for the elite, educated, and talented, which leaves them out. They do not trust their own judgments about art, leaving them to seek out the safest position—to just stay away from art. "Art is for other people, not me," is the conclusion. Could this be you?

What most people really want is to simply feel at ease with art activity, to enjoy art, which we have seen clearly enhances life for others. Some of us would like to restore the confidence we may have had in childhood, trust our own art decisions, and not feel bad about art anymore. Simply put, wouldn't you like to feel good about art again?

Many people think the problem is that they need to know more about art. I have often heard people say, "I don't know anything about art, but I know what I like." Have you ever thought that? It's easy to reason that "understanding" art somehow entitles one to indulge the art impulse, whether that means just being around art or enjoying the art of others and perhaps even purchasing art. It's easy to buy into what this author calls the Art Myth.

You might even end up not ever doing anything in the area considered art since you might feel it would reveal to others that you don't know anything about art. You might worry that you might get laughed at or become embarrassed if you chose or liked something that "the art snobs" think is silly. It feels like announcing our art preferences can reveal that the choice obviously came from an art-ignorant person. As an art-insecure person, you can become paralyzed by this fear of trusting your own aesthetic judgments. You can become hesitant when confronted with any art venture. Your life becomes a life without art.

The real problem is that you absolutely do know what you like. You are just too afraid to act upon your inner knowing, your instincts. The fear of looking foolish in the art world is too strong for you to buck those feelings and just enjoy art on your own terms. When you do not know what to do, the choice is to do nothing.

You may rationalize why art is not for you. Have you ever thought, "I can't draw," "I'm not creative," and well, why not conclude that "art doesn't matter that much anyway." Those rationales allow people to feel comfortable. You can then state, "I am just fine! Thank you." When art-insecure adults are faced with a potential art decision such as redecorating the house, many will choose to seek out and follow the opinion of art experts, choosing those "expert" decisions over their own likes and dislikes. Not trusting your instincts is costly.

The consistent mistrust of one's own art instincts undermines self-confidence generally, and not just around art. It just does not feel good to not like your own opinions. It seeps into everything about one's self-esteem. When we mistrust ourselves, we feel vulnerable and seek out authorities to authenticate our choices. It seems like a natural alternative.

What you need to do instead is to accept that these are old beliefs that came about in childhood, maybe in error. You need to understand that beliefs can change with new experiences. You must think that art awareness can enrich life in a safe and fun way and, finally, that changing beliefs is worth doing.

Life with art is just more fun and more stimulating, making daily activities more exciting. Trusting one's judgment strengthens future decisions and results, helping the once insecure adult enjoy life more fully. This, in turn, enriches all of society. Examining old beliefs that resulted from childhood thinking is not only worth doing; it's also not hard and very rewarding. It is the point of this book.

When it comes to art, you be the judge. Reawaken your instincts and enjoy art on your own terms.

CHAPTER I

A LIFE WITHOUT ART

HAVE YOU EVER FELT THAT ART JUST ISN'T FOR YOU? HAVE YOU EVER felt the need to excuse yourself for not being creative or artistic? Why did you feel that way? I notice those art insecurities in people all the time. Last night, I met a world-class cellist. When we talked about my being an artist, the first thing she said was, "I'm not creative!" I have often wondered why people feel they need to tell me that immediately. If I met an athlete or an actor, I would not feel obliged to tell them that I am not talented in that way. It is as if by announcing a weakness, it will not be discovered in the future and won't do us any harm. It seems to be a protective mechanism.

What is it about art that is so intimidating? Is it that people respect it *so* much or admire those who do it *so* much that they feel they need to explain they are not part of that tribe? Or is it that art has taken on the reputation that it is not for everyone? It is curious, isn't it? The best-kept secret is that art *is* for all of us. I am going to explore with you why people choose to leave art out of their lives. What does a life without art look like?

ART IS WITHIN US

I believe I was born to love art! But here's the thing: so were you! It is easy to see a child's innate love of all the arts. I once sent my three – and four-year-old nieces some little nylon net costumes for ballet dancing. I asked my sister if they liked them, and she said, "Oh, they're twirling all over the house!" They needed no instructions. They knew exactly how to be world-class dancers!

So, what happens to that innate art confidence as we grow up when it comes to the arts? This book will help you understand why you may be feeling inadequate about art judgments when they are presented to you.

I know you have heard it said, and perhaps you have said this yourself: "I don't know anything about art, but I know what I like." I maintain that, yes, indeed, *you do know what you like!* The great thing is you don't need to "know" any more about art. You have natural inborn art instincts that tell you what you like. After you read this book, you may want to change your statement when confronted with art to, "I already know all I need to know about art, and I know what I like!"

That's a more accurate statement. We will explore what happened to you and many other adults that made you hesitate to follow your own inclinations when it came to art and what to do about it. Let's get started.

WHAT DOES IT MEAN TO "KNOW" ART?

What do people mean when they talk about knowing art? "Knowing art" suggests that somehow people need to study something to enjoy it! I have known people who lost their enjoyment of music once they began to study musical theory. Analyzing something too closely can actually alter the way we perceive it and can override our intuitive responses. It is not necessary to know musical theory to enjoy music. Nor is it necessary when we look at art to understand all the motivations of the artist or the history, techniques, and processes. On the other hand, it is *fun* to know about what makes a work of art a work of art! Life should be fun!

There have been endless theories about the famous Leonardo da Vinci painting, the *Mona Lisa*. Why is she smiling? It is a fun exercise to ponder why she seems to be smiling. The question here, though, really is, does it matter? That painting is just a beautiful painting. We like looking at it. That is why it is a masterpiece, not because we know everything about it. Maybe it is the enigma of *why* she's smiling that speaks to our inner self.

If you have been using the excuse that you do not know enough about art to pursue it, this book should free you to put that notion aside. We will be talking about how to think differently about art in the future. As I have stated, you already know all you need to know about art to have it in your life! We don't have to study it.

YES, ART IS WITHIN US!

Have you ever gone around the corner and seen something and thought, *"WOW!! I LOVE THAT!"*? A pretty girl, a pretty car, a mountain? Then you know what I am talking about when I say you have instincts! You don't have to know anything about what is considered a pretty girl, a pretty car, or a mountain. Your inner self connects with what you see, right?

You are simply reacting to what you saw, and you trust your reaction. Should it be any different when faced with art objects? You have instincts for art, too, and we are going to discuss what they are and how they can help you from now on.

Let's begin with the assumption that these instincts for art are still within you, though they may be a bit rusty. We will discuss how to bring them back to life. Why? Because it is more fun when you can trust that when you say you love it, it is a fair enough judgment. We have built-in barometers about what we like. We have also learned not to trust those responses for a variety of reasons, which we will reveal. It is an interesting fact of education that once we consider the source of an idea, we can accept or reject that idea. So, let's also assume that art instincts can be reawakened by examining them. How will this book help you do that? By looking at old ideas from childhood that we may still hold true.

MY HOPE FOR THIS BOOK

This book is a treasury of personal conclusions I have come to through a lifetime of art producing, teaching, exhibiting, selling, advising, and critiquing. This is from the artist's point of view. It is not meant to be an academic treatise but, rather, a totally personal review of how honoring one's natural art awareness can enhance life. We will examine the role art plays in your life today. We will speculate as to what your life could look like if you changed your mind about including more art. You may find that it will open the door to a more satisfying daily life. Life without art is just not as rich.

I will illustrate my points as we go along, which will show you how my life as an artist evolved. As my friend says, "How does a tree become a tree?" I was lucky. I was allowed to follow my natural instincts and establish my own conclusions. Jacques Cousteau once said that he felt that if he knew something, he was obliged to tell others about it. I feel very much that way, and that is why I wrote this book.

I became a teacher; I taught art to every level of student. I became an art historian, and I was a museum administrator. I have continually been a working artist. I am currently in the three thousand number in my inventory of paintings produced and exhibited. I have devoted my life to the making and understanding of art. I now feel obliged to tell you what I have learned.

Throughout this book, I will be asking you for rapid responses to the ideas presented here. The first knee-jerk reaction is often the most astute. Write your reactions to the questions posed. Everyone knows it is always better to write things down as our minds cannot accurately retrieve every concept we hear about from memory. This book will serve as a journal. There are blank pages and specialized quizzes for you to note what you are learning. It's a workbook within a book. And it's a keeper.

Write in it, keep it, and refer to it. When you have finished this book, you should have a journal documenting your journey and the renewal of your art instincts. That is why it is worth keeping. It will become a testament to your art recovery.

We are going to describe concepts using thought exercises with places for your answers. You will have it written down in one place. At the end of the book, you should have a record of what you did, how you reacted, and what you liked and didn't like in confronting your beliefs about art. This is useful because when something is in black and white in front of us, we can often analyze it differently and better.

There will often be places for you to write your spontaneous reactions about what you are reading and, therefore, experiencing. These may sound repetitive at times. The idea here is that as you read, you will grow. The same question a few chapters ago may not, in fact, garner the same response in you this time around. This is the way we learn. It was pointed out to me once (by my sister) when I complained that I seemed to be coming back to the same point over and over. "Louise," she said, "you are not at the same point. Growth is not circling back to the same point on the same level. Growth is an upward spiral. You may revisit the same point, but now you are on a higher level!" Ah. That feels better, doesn't it? So, we will be spiraling upward on this art journey of yours with questions to spark your new thoughts, exhibiting the reawakening of your art instincts.

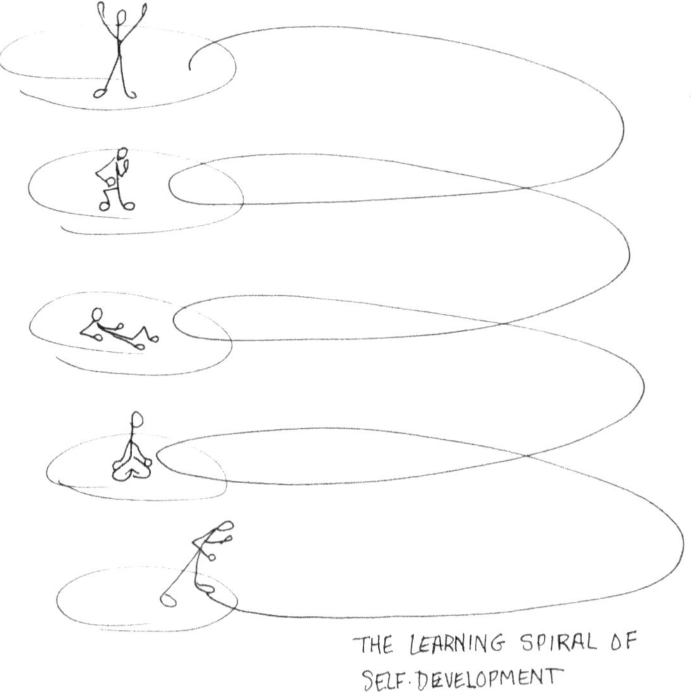

IT'S A JOURNAL FOR YOUR JOURNEY

Your journey is an ongoing, organic event that will keep you thinking and changing. So keep your writing tools and materials nearby as you experience different emotions while reawakening your art instincts. We are looking to document changes in thinking. That's the point: we are looking for change. We are looking for which ideas to keep and which ideas to reformat. We will be identifying art conclusions that are no longer as useful to us as they were in childhood. The result should be a thought-through belief system about art for you as an adult and not the random leftovers from childhood thinking that gave you your present system for processing art. This book is going to reflect that transformation.

We are going to talk about breaking the rules, and yes, you can write in the margins. This is a personal collection of your initial responses. It also can be a place to put notes about your ongoing growth. You will be led to an expansion of ideas that are going to let you daydream and plan. You will want to make notes to help you forget some old notions and make reminders to remember important concepts. So, dog-ear away.

I once visited the home of Carl Sandburg, the famous poet. I was amazed when I saw his library. There was not one book there that didn't have pages with corners turned down. It was refreshing to know that he, a famous poet, was bookmarking favorite thoughts from other sources. Do it, too; this is very helpful in self-development of any kind, as not only can you not remember everything, but when revisiting a concept, you will know more and get more from the notes.

Consider this book a forever resource for staying on the journey of recovering your Art Self.

Now, let's examine your starting point.

HOW DO YOU FEEL ABOUT ART RIGHT NOW?

Do you remember a time when you loved art?

Any kind of art?

At what age?

Do you remember the feeling? Describe it.

Did you know you were doing without your art instincts? Yes or no?

Does this resonate with you or sound true to you?

What if you reawakened these instincts?

Why do you think art is important to our lives at all?

WE TRUST WHAT WE SEE

VISUAL ART IS ALL AROUND US. WE EITHER LIKE OR DON'T like what we see. And we do trust our eyes to tell us the truth.

Because I am a visual artist, we are going to limit our discussion of your art instincts to visual art. It is what I know best. Often, it is what people think of when we say "art." For this discussion, we will address how people see the world and art around them. People respond to what they see in their world every day. People respond to paintings the same way as they do to everything else. It's just that when it is labeled "art," people think they should respond differently, that there is a formula for looking at art "right"! The fact that they think they should do that is what we are discussing here. Everyone in the developed cultures wonders what art really is. Is this true in the developing countries?

In a word, no. Everyone everywhere makes art. Everyone everywhere decorates their houses, whether it's a mud hut or a fancy chalet.

What is art anyway? Even experts can't agree on the elements of good and bad art, but that is not the question. Here, we want to discuss what we normally consider to be art. The one thing all people innately know is that art "speaks to us" on a gut level, and that brings us to a different definition than intellectuals would discuss.

ART IS SIMPLY COMMUNICATION—
WHEREVER YOU FIND IT

Art can be defined as the expression or application of human creative skill and imagination, typically in a visual form such as painting or sculpture, producing works to be appreciated primarily for their beauty or emotional power.

Art is communication through emotion. Even when you think you love a work of art because you understand its message logically, you are reacting to it emotionally first. Actually, art is simply communication on a gut level and not on an intellectual, knowledge-based level. Art expresses emotions. And that speaks to us on a primal level. There are many forms of art, and it is *always* communication through emotions. It's a sensory thing. We trust what our senses tell us. They seem reliable to us. A hot stove. Deep water. The sound of an alarm. We trust our senses.

Why do *you* think that people think they have to know about art to enjoy it?

FEELINGS BECOME THOUGHTS,
NOT THE OTHER WAY AROUND

Feelings become thoughts, not the other way around. Emotions enter our brains first, and then we form words and ideas around the pictures. We think in pictures first! That means instinct instead of intellect is a truer inner compass of the communication we feel when looking at art.

The challenge is that people have learned to think that art is logical and there are reactions we are *supposed* to have. Not true. That's why we don't need to "know" art before we can love it. Art is subjective. Art is personal. Do you see, then, how important it is to pay attention to what your instincts are telling you?

IS ART EVER LOGICAL?

We might choose to look at a piece of artwork because, intellectually, we are intrigued. Why did Andy Warhol paint Campbell's Soup cans, and why does that work hang in a museum? It doesn't make sense emotionally. Soup cans? Really? So, we might look at that idea to see if it resonates with us. We might read about Andy Warhol and his motivation. The truth of it is, however, that when you look at that work, and you love it or hate it, it is not because of what you "know" about it.

Since the inception of artificial intelligence, there has been the recognition that artificial intelligence, or AI, as it is called, is devoid of emotion. That is true, and what is the issue? We have always accepted that computers have no emotions. (And they don't get tired either.) However, computers can generate "art" that people will enjoy. Computer art will always speak to someone, somehow, *because of the emotions of the receiver.* This is true. This is especially true because of the use of color, to which all of us react.

If AI does not evoke emotion in us, it will feel shallow and tutorial rather than feel like a form of expression. That is the difference between when an artist puts paint on canvas and when a machine does it.

LOVING ART IS NATURAL

It is natural. It's not natural to need to "know about art" before you can enjoy it. It's not natural to stand before a painting and wonder, "What should I be thinking about this? I had better not tell anyone what I really think because 1) I'm probably missing something, 2) I am probably wrong, 3) They will laugh at me, and 4) I don't understand it. Should I understand it? What is it about, anyway?" And on and on and on.

That is not natural.

External forces have a lot to say about art. It must be stated that appreciating art is an internal job. One can appreciate a piece of music without ever wanting to hear it again. We honor the fact that someone put their heart and soul into composing the work; we intellectually respect that. However, if it does not "sing" to us, we don't like it. It is a visceral response. We feel the music. Either we like the feeling, or we don't. If we like it, we will want to hear it again. Forget it if we didn't like what we heard.

WHY HAVE ART IN OUR LIVES?

Why should we even care about art? In this chapter, we will uncover the ways in which art enriches life. Why art? Art has been proven to enrich lives; that's why! It's human nature to enjoy art. Engaging in art can make us happy.

We seek it all the time without meaning to because we yearn for expression—our own and that of others. Most people put art on the back shelf, leaving it for the time when they can study it, learn more about it, and then feel better about their art decisions. The issue becomes, why do we feel we need to know all about art to enjoy it? It is simply not true.

We have an innate calling to art. We just don't always call it art. Creativity is joyful and rewarding, and we deserve to experience it in our lives. We sometimes fear what makes us feel good; our own sense of unworthiness may interfere. Even early man found art satisfying. Simply said, art is communication. It is expression through emotion. There are many forms of art, but it is *always* communication through emotion. Therefore, all art is personal and subjective to each of us. Creativity and its products are our birthright; why should we do without them?

When people put art on the back shelf, leaving it for a time when they can study it, there may be other forces at work. Strangely, we fear we might not deserve what makes us feel good. That's too bad. Another hindrance to happiness in life.

Recovering your natural art instincts is a good thing, and here's why: *If* life is better with art in it, and *if* all people everywhere are looking for happiness, and *if* it's human nature to enjoy art, and *if* yearning for expression is born within us, *then* art can make us happy. But not if you continue to believe that art is not for you.

There is a cost to not using your natural art instincts. Living with doubt and art insecurity "colors" all of your life (excuse the pun). You live life differently when there is no engagement with art. A rich life includes some risk-taking; certainly, changing one's beliefs might feel risky. I would suggest here that one could almost call what we are going to do "safe risk-taking" (which sounds like an oxymoron). One of our objectives here is to take those baby-step risks that can feel safe and comfortable and still reach results.

CHAPTER 3

Art Instincts

Art instincts might be called art intuitions, Art DNA, or innate art intelligence. For this discussion, I am referring to those quiet signals in our brains that help us through life—our instincts—and as they refer to exposure to art (our art instincts). Art instincts are in all of us to seek out art. Art instincts can lead us to satisfaction if we learn to listen.

We all have instincts about everything. Thank goodness. Those emotional reactions help warn us against danger. We take care of ourselves instinctively. Generally, we protect our instincts, actually reinforcing them in our children. We think it is good to listen to ourselves; it helps us take care of ourselves. We seek out the things that are good for us and avoid those things that are not good for us. We are always looking for what makes us feel good.

This is very true about including art in one's life. Art makes us feel good. In today's society, however, no one is protecting our art instincts, and the message of what art is supposed to mean gets muddied. As adults, we get so confused about how we are supposed to react to art that we simply avoid it altogether. That is a shame.

There seems to be a natural, inborn craving for art in one's existence. This is especially obvious in children, not just when it comes to the decorative, environmental effect of art but also the making of all art. It has occurred since the dawn of man in all cultures everywhere on earth. It makes sense that the evolvement of humankind had to include art and creativity.

We will take a look at some examples later.

Do you remember a time when you loved art?

Any kind of art?

At what age?

Do you remember how it made you feel? Describe it.

Good news! Your art instincts are temporarily dormant, not permanently gone! What is there to gain by pursuing art again? Happiness.

HOW NOT TRUSTING YOUR ART INSTINCTS AFFECTS YOUR DAILY LIFE

As I have noted, people who no longer trust their innate judgment of art have altered their relationship to it. The art instincts children use are an important birthright. To not honor those instincts means to put art out of reach forever. That is a shame because art is such a joyful addition to daily life. I am sure it is not a conscious decision to look at art as something for others to enjoy. However, the consequences of somehow learning that art is only for a privileged few dictate that most people feel their relationship with art is limited.

How does this happen? I think it comes from well-meaning adults. Why would anyone take away the joy children feel when exposed to art? It is not intentional. Well-meaning adults sometimes make a casual remark to a child that changes that child's perception forever. Adults are supposed to influence children. Children are taught to respect their adult influences and learn from them. If you think of the most important adults in a child's life, parents are the number one influence. The parental voice is just stronger than anyone else's. All of us seek parental approval, and when our parents say something about anything, we believe them. And we change our behavior.

This is mostly a good thing. A society needs the civilizing of children to make a responsible human group. Children are so uninhibited in everything they do that rules need to be set and followed. I plan to show you here the unintended results of the voices of other influences on us as children. Consider teachers, club leaders, other children, siblings, people at church, and all other societal adult influences and how they affect our thinking. And more importantly, our emotions.

Can you see how this can happen to children? It is innocently done. As I have said, people don't set out to maliciously take joy from others by making them fearful of their art choices. It happens inadvertently. If you think about it, you may have an incident in your childhood when a respected adult authority in your life let you know where you stood when it comes to art.

I, myself, was challenged as a child about my art abilities. It was a confusing episode in my life when I was ten years old. There was a poster contest in my school, and I wanted to see if I could win it. It was to be a *hand-drawn* poster (I don't remember the details of the rules except that one). I bought a piece of poster board, and my mother let me stay up until 11 p.m. drawing Disney comic characters all around the edges. I made those crayons sing! It turned out great! And I knew I had won! I couldn't wait to hear my name spoken over the loudspeaker so everyone would know I had won. When they announced the winner, I was stunned to find it was not me! I knew mine was the best. How could this be? Someone else had won the prize?

I was so motivated to find out why I hadn't won that I marched my little self to the school office to get an explanation. "Why didn't I win?" I asked. "Clearly, you traced it!" the lady said with stern authority. What was I to do? There was no changing the outcome. I was baffled. I thought, "This was the reward? It was *too* good? How could that be?"

I never forgot the feeling of those adults' mistrust of my intentions. I was appalled that they thought I had cheated. Even at ten, I had integrity, and it hurt my feelings that they thought that I had done that. Instead of this being a positive attempt at making art, as it was supposed to be, it became an example of having done something wrong. I didn't understand how it could even happen. That incident eventually steeled my resolve to follow my own instincts and be wary of the judgment of others.

HOW DO I KNOW SO MUCH ABOUT ART INSTINCTS? I have taught all types of art to all ages in many different ways and in many different settings. In speaking to my young audiences of children, I realized that the parents or teachers in the back of the room were riveted by what I was teaching, wanting to learn about art even at about a third-grade level. *"Why is that?"* I wondered. I later learned that researchers in art education have found in that between third and fourth grade, children decide whether or not they can draw. Some of the reasons for this are physical, as eyesight and other maturing factors have their effects. Somehow, over that summer, they can see that what they see and what they draw do not match. It is that realization that tells them that some kids are talented (their drawings look better) and "some of us" are not. Reality takes away that confidence in fantasy we had at birth.

I began to realize that the very interested adults in the back of the room were picking up where they had left off. They had put art aside because they thought it was not for them. Now, they wanted to experience art as adults without inhibition, and were eager to be as enthusiastic as the young children were. They were third graders again and eating it up! They became open to art again. It was a safe place to learn, to be in a room with young children listening to what the adults had left behind. They loved it, and I loved it.

SEE IF YOUR INSTINCTS KICK IN
WHEN YOU READ THIS

I think I was about twenty years old when I discovered haiku. This wonderful ancient Japanese poetry form is based on expressing a whole story in seventeen syllables. I am not sure how or where I learned the one that sticks in my mind the most. See if you like it too.

> *There in the garden . . .*
> *Going row to row . . .*
> *Stitching . . . stitching . . .*
> *Butterflies!*

Can't you just see them? The words bring up an image that is so familiar to us. It touches us. The poem paints a picture for us to see. It expresses that joy we feel when we uncover a wonderful surprise in nature. It just feels good. It makes us happy. And we don't have to know anything about art to love it. Or butterflies. We instinctively know all we need to know.

That instant reaction to the picture is natural. That is the child in us still loving surprises. Have you ever seen a child using a stick as a wand dancing in a garden, anointing plants as she goes? Or a child wielding a stick, sword fighting an imaginary foe in the garden? Those kinds of instinctual dances children do don't have anything to do with formal dancing as an art except joy.

See how those facts, those internal feelings, conflict with the statement, "I don't know anything about art, but I know what I like"? You do, too, know everything you need to know about art. Art is instantly recognizable to the child within us.

All people gain feelings through sound, touch, and vision. When you read the haiku poem, you had an emotional reaction, right? You have been in a setting where butterflies flit from one plant to another. The feeling that they are stitching rows together is a nice idea and a very poetic conclusion, but the emotion communicated comes from the joy that butterflies always bring us. They symbolize joy in a way. They are so lighthearted, it seems, just looking pretty all the time. It makes us happy to connect with that joy. It is not the intellectual wording of the poem but the emotions the words fire up. The words reminded us of those feelings. That is successful art!

In all transparency, this haiku was either made up by me long ago, or I learned it so early I don't remember the source. There is a haiku about butterflies that the haiku poet Master Bashi's student, Kawai Sora crafted, portraying butterflies as "weaving." "Back and forth, through rows of wheat, a butterfly weaving." Perhaps I saw that and changed the wording. I know it has stuck with me all these years as an example of pure emotion through pictures painted with words. Wonderful.

CHAPTER 4

Awareness Is Key to Recovery

What will it take to get our art instincts back? First, we have to acknowledge that we have lost our inborn instincts when it comes to art and that recovery is valuable to us. Awareness is key. There will be art awareness play suggestions later in the book. There are some new ways of thinking; all you have to do is change your mind. Playing with new ideas does that.

How can I get my art instincts back?

1. Start looking at art again with new eyes; I will teach you how.
2. Discover old notions you learned growing up that are now keeping you from enjoying art and erase them.
3. Exercise new ways of seeing; practice playing with that idea.
4. Develop new paths of art enjoyment; explore new ways to see, not just look.
5. Repeat.

Is it hard to find our way back to our childhood instinctual love of art?

Not at all, it just takes practice, going back to the play you used to enjoy, and finding the fun in art again.

Can I do it overnight?

If you want to. An aha moment can make change instantaneous. Or take two days—more if you want. This is all at your natural pace; you navigate your journey. Are you in? GOOD! Let's go!

ART AWARENESS: HOW CAN I GET SOME?

Since it's clear that art awareness will lead us to the goal of loving art again, first, we must practice noticing art. We have to acknowledge that art is all around us, everywhere, all the time. Taking that as a fact, you are most likely looking at art every day without realizing it. It's time to wake up! We are not talking about a 24-7 effort, by the way! Just conscious moments of awareness, which, with practice, can enhance viewing life differently.

There are some environments where awareness is always heightened. For instance, race car driving is an intense spectator sport. It is an art event! Full of color and texture and certainly lots of loud sounds and lots of forms of sensory touch for the audience. All the spectator's senses are alive! The sense of touch goes further than actual, physical touch. We say sometimes, "It touched me." Visual art is surely a form of touch, just like live music, a massage, a person whispering, or being barefoot in the sand. These are all examples of experiences with touch. When we see something that seems to us to be "touching," it evokes emotions that are very direct communications with our inner selves. That is art speaking to us. We just don't usually call it that. Most people would not call race car driving an art event. But it is. Anything with that much color and texture is an art event. It's very visually stimulating. We will further explore why visual art is a form of touching.
What do you enjoy presently that is basically an art experience? Do you dance? Do you build sandcastles? Do you play with your food? Do you fiddle with the paint chip colors at the store?

As we said, paying attention to your present activities can be a guide to some art awareness activities already going on in your life. Name some.

Are you beginning to see how comprehensive art really can be? It is not just one thing but, rather, a sensation from everything, intentionally or not, in our environment.
Use this space to recall a time when you were touched by something unexpectedly.

How did that feel?

How would you describe that communication? Joyful? Amazing? Comforting? Profound?

Would you be open to another experience like that?

Get ready!

THE PAYOFF WHEN YOUR OLD ART INSTINCTS ARE WORKING AGAIN

The good news is that as you start to work on your own internal art awareness and rebuild some basic premises about art, you will naturally collect evidence to prove to yourself that, indeed, you can. You will be able to love your art instincts again and trust your judgment. It's a fact. You will love recognizing that little voice that says, *"Wow! Look at that!"*

The payoff when your old art instincts are working again is you get your old friend, freedom, back! It comes back! Childhood freedom! That is worth fighting for. Don't you get jealous when you see children enjoying their freedom every day? We typically resent it. As adults, we have resigned ourselves to a life of constraint, and children show no holding back!

With freedom, you get to make choices that you really like, which feels joyful. You get to get rid of Granny's old stuff you never did like. You have more options—put it in storage or give it away to someone who loves it. I know this seems like heresy and disrespect to Granny at first, but yes, you can throw it away without feeling insecure. You can have the freedom to choose to own *only* what you like. Think about it! Imagine how that might feel. Every time you pass that spot, and you no longer must look at that old table, you will feel an inner glow of satisfaction. Think of how it will feel when you have cleared a space that used to feel so crammed with stuff you never wanted in the first place. It's a lovely feeling to be surrounded only by things that bring you joy. Art brings joy.

TRUST YOUR ART CHOICES

Since all instincts are within us throughout our lives, it is reasonable to think we can recover the ones obliterated by old beliefs when it comes to art. With one caveat: *You can set up new "shoulds" while trying to remove old ones!*

We are just human. Not everything is perfection. Let's not look for the perfect result when moving forward with this journey. It is easy to replace one set of guidelines with another. I'm sure you have seen it happen with food! That food has been determined to be bad for your health, only to find in thirty years it is the best food on the planet—eggs! The objective here is not to find absolute truths about art, except one. Do you want it in your life? Do you like it? You may be comfortable with just having "stuff" around you every day—for some, it's comforting to be surrounded by stuff, any kind of stuff. That's okay. To just have stuff around because you never considered it, however, is an interesting option.

The buzzword going forward in considering art is *awareness*. As we have said, all decisions are okay as long as you are conscious that you are making them. Most people simply drift into the life they live. There's a certain freedom in not having to choose, if that's what you want. One of your goals here is to be conscious of your choices. We are going to discuss having the freedom to make different choices without restrictions. We are not going to enforce new rules about how to live but instead rely upon our good instincts.

Others who are not interested in recovering art instincts may not understand your new outlook. Actually, you don't even have to explain any of this to them. It is only for you. You chose this book instinctively because something in it spoke to you. That is a good enough reason to pursue a new approach to art. Keep it quiet so you can enjoy the journey without thinking of the judgment of others.

Art is a magic potion; it will make changes in you, regardless of whether you give it the power to do so. It is wonderful to have things in your environment that give you joy just by being there. Like a good souvenir, it may just bring about happiness because you like it.

RECOVERY

Recovering art instincts simply means paying attention to your reactions. Going through life in a numb state without ever noticing your environment, ignoring your feelings, and not paying attention to art is limiting. Just wait until you feel awake again because you have started to notice art around you! It is going to feel great! Isn't it time you brought your childlike wonder back into daily life? It is not that hard. Use the following space or a separate journal to begin trying!

Do you commit now to change your views about yourself and art and your life and art?

Aren't you curious to see if you can do better?

Don't you need a feeling of validation about your art instincts?

How long has it been since you felt like your old feelings about art are still true?

Don't you wish you had the freedom a child has to simply want and get?

It's an easy formula for happiness! And the feelings of freedom are the key—the secret.

WOMEN HAVE WINGS!

Many years ago, I became interested in single-line drawing. I was completely fascinated in college, watching my teacher, the great Italian artist, John DeMartelli describe the human figure in one line. Drawing an entire composition with a single line where the pen never leaves the paper is a challenge. I loved the idea that you had to know where you were going without hesitation. If you stop or lift the pen, it creates a blob of ink or a gap in the line, which disturbs the flow of it. That was unacceptable!

There seemed to be a life to those drawings that was exciting. That is reminiscent of the Chinese notion of the life-force known as Chi, which is believed to be present in all things. It was thrilling to draw with a single line and do it well. I got better and better at it; it became easier and easier to do it successfully.

It did feel like the lines had Chi in them. People instantly took to them. I drew figures tumbling one into another across an entire page or canvas in all kinds of attitudes and gestures. I kept this up for many, many years. In 1976, I drew a series of line drawings for a book that I called *Lifelines*. It exists today in the Library of Congress.

I still draw lifelines because they seem to express my view of people and what they are feeling.

I had been looking for a simple way to express feelings. The single-line drawing technique fulfilled the requirements perfectly. Could I show a person in a relaxed pose, with feet up, sitting in a lounge chair? Yes. Could I show the joy of dancing in one line? Yes. Could it be that all emotions could be portrayed this way? Yes! I was intrigued. I was hooked.

I always wanted to reach all people with my art, so my figures took on a birdlike shape. It seems that nearly everyone likes birds. Birds seemed to me to be ecumenical and a nondiscriminatory way to show a figure. If it had no face but a beak-like head shape, it wasn't identified with a specific type of human. When I added wings instead of arms, the figures had no gender. With a beak and wings, everyone could relate to the images just as we do to birds. People felt the feelings of having wings. We would like to fly like that, right?

At the time, I was also very engaged in my own emergence as a woman artist trying to find and exercise my power. I was also very aware of the evolution of women's rights in the sixties, and the figure seemed to portray a woman emerging as her soaring self. If I added breasts, there was no doubt now that this was a female, birdlike shape who had found and was using her wings. This type of drawing became symbolic to me of girls becoming women, women finding their wings, and the notion that we have a natural inner desire to fly. Once we acknowledge our power, the sky is the limit!

I wanted women to see that they oversee their own empowerment, which is another message of this book. Women instinctively know about creation because they can give birth to another life. I want women to know that creativity exists for them in all areas of their personal growth.

The birdlike single-line figures became my haiku, a strong thought simply stated and immediately recognized by the audience.

Here is an example of my woman with wings after she has discovered she *has* wings, her joyful self showing the world

she can do anything. It is also now, to me, a symbol of all wom-
en who have recognized their creative powers.

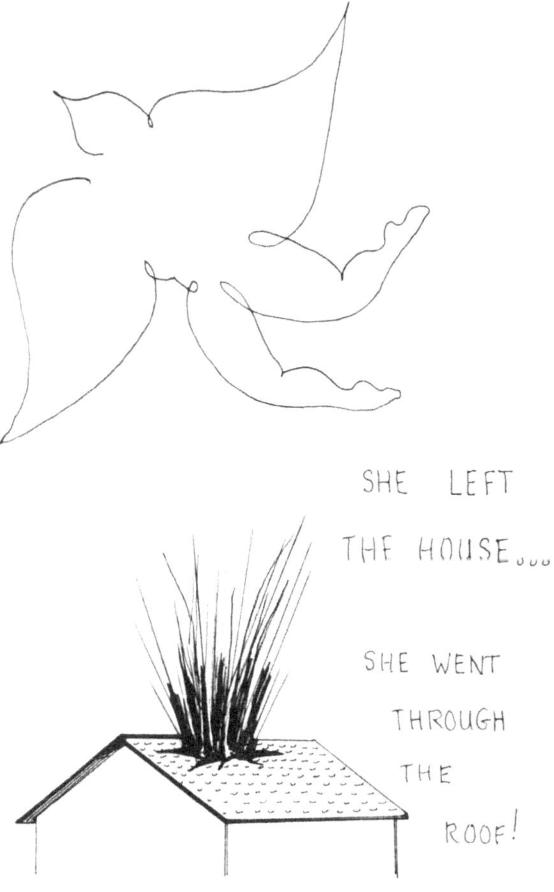

Here she is! Can you relate? Do you recognize the feeling
she expresses? Haven't you felt that way too? Let's get that
feeling back into your daily life more often; there's a lot of daily
joy out there.

CHAPTER 5

What Happened to Our Art Instincts?

The art instincts children naturally use are an important birthright. To not honor those instincts means to put art out of reach forever. We have said that is a shame, since art is such a joyful addition to daily life. I am sure it is not a conscious decision to look at art as something for only others to enjoy. The consequences of somehow believing that art is for a privileged few are only mandates to most people that their relationships with art must be limited.

How did this happen? Why would anyone take away the joy children feel when exposed to art? It is not intentional. Well-meaning adults sometimes make a casual remark to a child that changes that child's perception forever. Notice I said "well-meaning adults." It is the unintended result of careless remarks or adult reactions we are addressing here. Adults are supposed to influence children. It's their job. Children are taught to respect their adult influences and learn from them. If you think of the most important adults in a child's life, parents are the number one influence. The parental voice is just stronger than anyone else's. All of us seek parental approval, and when they say something about art, we believe them. Then we change our behavior for parental approval. This is natural.

This is mostly a good thing. A society needs the civilizing of children to make a responsible human group. Children are so uninhibited in everything they do that rules need to be set and followed. I plan to show you here the unintended results of the voices of other influences on us as children. Consider teachers, club leaders, other children, siblings, church leaders, and all other societal adult influences and how they affect our thinking and, more importantly, our emotions.

The trouble is that well-meaning adults often give the same weight to everything they say to a child. The child has to pay equal attention to "Here's how you hold a fork!" as to "Get out of the way! A truck is coming!" Children take it all seriously if they respect the authority of the adult.

By way of example, I have heard adults say, "That's not the way it looks!" or, "Shouldn't it be bigger?" or, "I've never seen one like *this* before!" or, "What made you use that color?" or, "I can't even tell who that is supposed to be." You can see how this might hurt art confidence in a child. When it happens enough times (which can be just a few incidents for a very sensitive child), the conclusion for that child must be that they are not good enough at art to pursue it any further. The damage is done by a well-meaning adult who inadvertently crushed an art spirit.

The criticism does not even have to be words said to them. Children can intuit your reactions emotionally from your body language. Remember, their instincts are alive and well. I have seen a parent accept a child's drawing and immediately rotate it around and around. It is very obvious to the child that the drawing is not clear enough for the adult to even know which way is up. The child must conclude that the drawing is terrible— he can't draw—or the adult would immediately see it as correct. Art is not for him.

A better way is to look over the child's shoulder, stand behind them, and camouflage your first feelings. Be delight- ed with everything. Children are not looking for conversation about the work, even if it is not their work being judged. Refrain from a discourse on what art should be. Ban from your vocabulary the words, "What is it?" If you really can't tell, ask a question and get a story out of the child for context instead. I have heard adults eloquently describe what could have been better if only the child had . . . insert here any number of artificial rules that most adults can't do either. It hurts a child's self-esteem and causes confusion and, ultimately, failure. It is better to just say, "Tell me about this." They will tell you the story and why they did what they did.

ART INSECURITY EXISTS ONLY IN ADULTS

The insecurity that people feel about art only occurs in adults. Children would never say such a thing as, "I don't know about art." All three-year-olds are certain about art. They love it; it is great! It is fun! They have no reason to justify any of their very positive feelings about art. Ever.

As we have acknowledged, somewhere in the process of growing up, children learn that art is not for everyone. They learn to believe that art is only for those who are talented, educated, rich, or somehow part of the Art Elite. I am calling this the Art Myth. I will discuss the many ways this is promoted, why, and the devastating results for society.

At this stage of my life, I have a long story of seeing that people are reluctant to lean on their own judgment. Many so-called experts have contributed to the myth that art is mysterious, complicated, and only for the educated. Why, then, are there courses that say, "Anyone can learn to draw"? I know this to be true, by the way. I believe anyone can learn to draw. Unless you cannot "draw" your name with a pencil, as in writing your name, you are most likely able to learn the techniques of drawing. Writing means that your eyes and hands work to make symbols (letters). Writing is a form of drawing. Even if it is not the most glorious handwriting, the fact remains that you can make letters signify your name. You can draw by learning techniques just as you learned to form letters.

The same goes for painting. Remember how joyful it was as a child to finger-paint? Or just grab a brush and put an image on a piece of paper? Not hard, right? And not intimidating.

That is until you decided, or someone decided for you, that you were not an artist. Children do not obey false and artificial "rules" about making and enjoying art in the beginning. Society teaches them to think differently about the process.
Can you think of a time when art was discouraged in your young life? Describe it.

List some beliefs that were handed down to you about art (Too expensive? Not necessary? Great for those who can do it? Can't make a living doing that! etc.).

HERE'S HOW CHILDREN FEEL ABOUT ART (UNIVERSALLY!)

Children love life itself joyfully. They accept all their feelings and have no trouble expressing them. Adults are not often able to "liberate" their emotions as freely as children do. You know children don't care what they express or where they express it. You know that is true! They cry, they yell, they scream, they stomp their feet, they throw tantrums! That's what they are feeling in the moment.

We know that to live in a civilized society, we must have rules, and we freely give those rules to our children. Unfortunately, by "civilizing" children, we suppress a lot more emotions than may be good for human expression. The baby gets thrown out with the bath water. However, along with undesirable behavior going out in the garbage, so also goes our natural art instincts. And that's not fair. It's not fair because of the value of expression and the joy self-expression brings to everyday life. Preserving open expression of emotion must be key. Many a marriage would be better with some open communication and expression of real feelings. Preserving expressive outlets for us as a society is beneficial in many ways.

Do you remember being expressive as a child? Overly expressive? Shy and not expressive?

What were you told about being expressive?

What was your favorite art activity when you were a kid?

Do you miss it?

Why?

THE POWER OF THE PARENTAL VOICE

I have said that whatever a parent says to a child has more weight to it than any other voice. That child will carry those words all through life. Parents do not mean to inhibit their children's love of art. Most parents who do this do it inadvertently. We must teach children the rules of life. Sometimes, it is not acceptable to scream and cry in church or some other place of reverence where quiet is important. Maybe the library is that sacred place where you just cannot express all your feelings in an outburst. There are other people to consider as well.

When we get rid of some of those uninhibited feelings in our children, we also place restrictions and inhibitions on their natural love of art. That great confidence that children have when they think they can do anything is a large sacrifice. It's a real disservice to children when they become insecure about art instead of just enjoying it.

How did your parents feel about art?

Did how they felt about art feel good or bad to you?

Older siblings are very influential to the younger children in a family. How did your siblings feel about art?

How did your older siblings feel about *your art?*

How did your parents feel about your art?

What did other influencers in your childhood feel about art?

Teachers? Friends? Care providers? Church directors? Peers? Note someone who stands out as being the most encouraging about art.

Note someone who stands out as being the most discouraging about art.

OTHER WELL-MEANING ADULT INFLUENCES ON CHILDREN

Let's talk about the unintended results of the voices of other influences on us as children. Consider teachers, club leaders, other older children, siblings, church organizers, and all other societal adult influences on us and how they affect our thinking—more importantly, how they affect our feelings. We are always learning from others. As we grow up, we learn to be more discerning about who we listen to and accept as authorities. However, children are taught to respect their elders and don't have as much choice about what influences them. Part of children's charm is their innocence, and in this case, it becomes a vulnerability.

People have asked me how I made my son so creative. My standard answer has always been, "I didn't make him creative! He came to me that way! I just wouldn't let anyone step on it!" I was very protective of his right to be imaginative. We will talk more about this later with some suggestions about protective parenting, providing freedom, and encouraging creativity.

In contrast to children, who are naturally open to everything, we must remind adults that they also had the same instincts when they were children and that the feelings about art are still inside them somewhere. This is the belief we will work on in this book. For our future, we should remember we can protect the children around us by being a little more careful with rules and regulations, as well as how we state them. By doing so, adults can perhaps cause less damage to children's need for expression. More about this later.

Can you think right now of an instance when you were discouraged from pursuing art?
Describe it.

CHILDREN ARE TAUGHT TO LISTEN

We all want to be acknowledged for being good. We crave validation. When it occurs, we cherish it. Every small win for us as a child builds confidence and well-being. When confidence in our own art enjoyment begins to erode, it spirals into the insecurities I have seen in many adults. Mainly, they feel that their art judgment cannot be trusted because they "don't know anything about art." I am here to tell you again that those childhood instincts are still there. Those childhood instincts can be trusted. You already know all you need to know about art.

I wanted to write this book to let you know that your confidence in your own art instincts can be reawakened. It is not even that hard. The first step is only knowing that it can be done. Art instincts (like other instincts) are simply dormant. They can be awakened through simple steps to build awareness that you are still a child inside, with the easy ability to love art again.

You most likely have some pet phrases you use when you encounter art. Some folks remind themselves that they really don't care about art. It's not that important to daily life, after all. Some immediately bring to life old memories of when they tried their hardest and were humiliated or shamed for their apparent lack of good art judgment.

Do you say the same thing over and over to let others know your feelings about art? To get out of having to experience more art or to show up at the play or the local art fair?

I don't really think art is that important!
We haven't any space in our house for art objects.
I'm not interested in art.
Art's expensive.
I don't know any good artists.
My friend buys art, and he doesn't know anything!
I can't believe people spend money on that stuff.
We have too much stuff already!

You know the kinds of sentiments I am driving at here . . . what do you say to yourself to let yourself off the hook (when your friend wants you to go to the flea market, consignment shop, art gallery, auction, etc.)?

I have asked a lot of people, "When did you decide you were not an artist?" The answers and tales they have told are devastating—just awful stories of art teachers who took pride in standing a young boy in front of the class with his drawing so they could make fun of it. Can you imagine this person would ever think he could be in the art world? Why would he ever take a risk into art again after that?

Over and over, I have heard stories about terrible casual comments that ruined a kid's self-esteem when it came to art. This proved to me that it is common, hurtful, and unforgettable to a child. The obvious conclusion for children is just to leave that subject alone. It's the beginning of the belief that art is not for them. They can't trust themselves anymore.
Can you think right now of another instance when you were discouraged about art? Describe it.

Here is the most common response I received when I asked adults to think of a time when they felt bad about art. Without hesitation, people could relate a specific negative incident. The conflict is that your adult mind knows the truth; the child in you is still hurt by that incident. There are many reasons a child's work looks like it was made by a child, the main one being it was made by a child! Adults, however, seem to want to "correct" it. We will talk more about this later in the book. For now, let's just imagine how great it would be to erase such a memory.
Did you know you had lost your art instincts?

This is an important question because we know that all recovery begins with the acknowledgment that the problem exists. Describe whether or not you think you feel the same about art as you did when you were a child.

What do you think happened?

Would you like to reawaken some of the joy you may have felt as a child?

What would that feel like?

Would it make a difference in the way you live your life?

CHAPTER 6

ART INSECURITIES

WHEN I BECAME A COLLEGE PROFESSOR TEACHING DESIGN and art history, I realized how desperately people wanted to "understand" art so they could enjoy it! I thought it was a disconnect in logic and a negation of emotion. I was intrigued even though I thought I understood their motivation. They wanted to be able to defend their aesthetic choices.

Teaching design, I saw how inhibited people had become, not trusting what simply looked good to them. They needed answers about *why* something appealed to them. They wanted rationales to defend their art choices.

Then I noticed that college students wanted to be sure they were going to be part of the Art Elite, so they studied art principles. Hard! *Hmmm . . . is that really the function of art?* I thought. Really? To become part of an elite group? What is art supposed to do anyway? Isn't it just for our enjoyment? What was all this study for anyway? Wasn't it just supposed to enrich? Or was the objective to gain status? The students didn't even realize what they were doing.

Yielding to our fears can feel good, secure, and safe. Everyone likes the comfort of security. I decided that what I was seeing college kids do in class every day was build reassurance and confidence that they knew art so they could always defend their judgments. They overstudied to make sure they got to a pseudo-superior level so no one could challenge them. I wondered if they knew what they liked without looking it up!

I soon discovered that knowing all about art so no one can argue with the judgment is what many adults want. Let's explore the payoff in continuing what I call the Art Myth. Sometimes, I call it the Elitist Art Myth because that is what it is.

AS A WORKING ARTIST, I SAW ART INSECURITY IN MANY ADULTS

I had many encounters with the public as I pursued my career as an artist. An easy avenue into selling one's work is to show artwork at street fairs. Local art fairs, exhibitions at community centers, and other staged art events gave me the chance to talk to people. The street fair environment somehow loosens people up, so they become very frank. They look at the work and then speak to the artist as if the work was not created by them. I found this fascinating. The public was brutal, uninhibited, and very informative.

As an aspiring artist, I wanted to hear their comments, whether positive or negative. I felt that their honest opinion helped me hone my craft. It is easy to fool oneself, but not the public. I learned about adult art insecurity that way. People seemed hesitant to commit even when they loved something.

Exhibiting my artwork at street fairs was an amazing education about the public's reaction to art. Sometimes, they went on the attack. A woman once said to me, "What were you thinking when you made this?" People could be quite rude when speaking about the work, as if the artist was not standing right there. Muttering comments about their own interpretation caused me to acquire a thick skin. I reminded myself that it was only their opinion. That helped me not take it all personally. If one does, it can be quite discouraging to even the most undaunted art spirit. I had to shield myself against feeling insecure about my own work. I worked to trust my own art judgments. My self-talk had to help me put on the armor it was going to take to be a real artist for the rest of my life. I had to be my own best friend and encourage, not discourage, myself while exposing my artist's soul on canvas to the public. It was challenging. I feel I prevailed because I was unwilling to sacrifice my dream.

Even though I am a very confident person, especially when it comes to my art abilities, I was often hurt by comments. Learning not to let those thoughtless comments get to me was an important part of my development as a successful artist.

I learned a lot by exhibiting my work at local fairs. The entire time I have exhibited my work, I've kept my prices affordable because I have also believed that people's taste and their pocketbooks don't always match. I loved the idea that people could enjoy art without spending an unreasonable amount of money. I took cost out of the equation, hoping to help people have the artwork they wanted.

If cost was not the issue, my reasoning went, then it was something else stopping people from taking the work home. I will add here that I did sell a lot of work. What caused some people's self-doubt to be so strong that they would deny themselves something they loved? Reinforcing my confusion about the reticence some showed was the fact that, often, people came back to get the piece having regretted not buying it in the first place. This observation added to my conclusion that people could not trust their own judgments. They were afraid.

STUDIO SHOWS SHOWED ME PEOPLE'S ART INSECURITY AGAIN!

For ten years, I would have art shows in my studio twice a year to exhibit my work. I would choose a theme on which to paint for six months and produce paintings, continually exploring and pushing that theme every day. By Mother's Day, I would have a large inventory, which I could clear out in a weekend show. In another six months, I would produce another show's worth of themed pictures in time for the holidays. I would have a hundred people come to my shows. It was a great way for me to grow.

Interestingly, people would come because my studio was in my house. First, they were curious about an artist's studio. More importantly, they felt safe. It was not a formal, elitist environment. I had never liked being a commodity for a gallery. A good gallery will promote an artist working in a narrow genre. There was always less freedom for me in that because I like switching themes. A gallery cannot afford to promote a portrait artist to fame who suddenly decides to paint landscapes. This, along with a 50–60 percent commission fee, prompted me to ask everyone I knew if they liked art and if they would like to come to my art show.

HOW MY PRIVATE ART SHOWS WORKED

First, they would come for the wine and cheese. I always made my studio shows a high-class affair (I have dozens of wine glasses). They loved bringing the family by to see what I did as an artist. They would ask me all sorts of questions about how the piece was made and why. They loved validating their initial response of being immediately intrigued by a work of art by discussing it with me. The second time attending a show, they would ask for that piece they had loved the first time. "Nope, sorry." It had been sold. The third time, they would bring the Bridge Club. I sold a thousand works of art this way. Everyone grew in their appreciation of art because it was easy.

They loved, and I loved, the casualness of the affair. They could come by while out running errands. It was not an intimidating exposure to art; it was easy, and the work was accessible. It was a safe place to explore art with very little risk. I would let them take a painting home (for free) and pay me later. No one ever stiffed me, because they loved the work. Another benefit was that I have been very fortunate in knowing my art patrons personally. I knew they bought the work because they loved the work. They told me so.

These types of shows are good for artists and certainly good for novice art collectors. If there is an event like this near you, consider dropping in for a glass of wine. You will be glad you did. This is one thing I know: you will learn something about yourself and art. New exposure to art (of any kind) is always enriching, even if you don't like the work itself. You cannot help but be affected; your emotions will tell you so.

In my case, the series of shows I did with the public strengthened my conclusion that people have an innate curiosity for and magnetism toward art. People do know what they like; it's all about the fear that their choices aren't right somehow.

THE COST OF NOT TRUSTING YOUR INSTINCTS WHEN IT COMES TO ART

When you cannot trust yourself to make aesthetic judgments, it costs you in all sorts of ways. Literally. We learn to rely on (and pay for) expert advice when the ultimate decision could have come from our own judgment. You probably do not think you make aesthetic decisions, but I insist you do it every day. I have long criticized education for not equipping people with basic skills essential in adult life. There are many needed skills that are ignored, such as financial and wealth education, relationship-building education, and conflict resolution, and certainly, aesthetic decision-making is one of them. How are you supposed to pick out the drapes you want in your house without trusting your own judgment?

Get an expert. Call in an interior decorator. Now, before you think I am down on interior decorators, I assure you I am not. I think they are great to bring to you all the merchandise options available when you are looking for new drapes. The main thing, though, is to keep the ultimate decision for you and you alone to make. How? By just choosing what you like. Your instincts will tell you at that moment that you like something enough to live with it. If you buy drapes you do not love because the expert thought it was the best choice, you are not being true to yourself. You have surrendered to the myth that others know what is best for you beyond your own gut reaction. Go with your gut. Hire the decorator to present choices, and then you choose. Art is so personal and subjective that there is no greater authority than you.

I love experts; do not get me wrong! Just because I think we have art intelligence inside us that guides us every day to what we love to look at does not mean I think we should never ask the experts. I also believe in lifelong learning. However, here is what is wrong with using experts: We give our authority away. If we defer to the judgment of the expert instead of having the final say on what we want to occur, we are mistrusting our own instincts and betraying the intuition to be true to ourselves. I do not believe we have law intelligence, for instance. I do believe if you need an interpretation of the law, you should consult an attorney.

Here is another way to think about it. Let that expert bring you all the options they can think of that might fit your needs.

But then, *YOU* decide which you like best. You do not have to defend your choice either. You hire them. They do the work. You use your decision-making ability to choose what you like best. You get the result you want. Easy, right?

I have known people who have lived for years with choices that the designer thought looked perfect. Never mind that it did not reflect the personalities of the owners. Why do we do that to ourselves? (I think you are beginning to understand why.)

Do we just carry our overly huge respect for authority into adulthood, and so we are afraid to stand up for ourselves? I maintain that, yes, we do just that. We are taught that the experts are right. We conclude that, after all, they have studied the subject and have more experience. However, just because the landscaper thinks that bush would look best here, if you do not like it there, don't put it there. Simple confidence in ourselves is the answer.

THE SQUELCH TEST

Are you inventing new ways to squelch your instincts? We can "pile on" when it comes to adding to negative beliefs for ourselves. Let's examine here what you think others did to your approach to art now.

How badly do you think your art instincts were squelched?

Identify feelings about childhood restriction of instincts (not situations, necessarily, but feelings).

Describe your feelings about art now after thinking some of this through.

What could change?

Do you want to change?

Is there anyone talented around you that makes you feel bad? Are you jealous? Are they?

Have you been bullied or intimidated when it comes to art? By whom?
 Is that person still around?

Do you think you have hidden potential to make art?

Do you suspect you might have been "talented"?

Even if you don't think you might have been talented, couldn't you still make art?

What's stopping you?

Who's stopping you? (Spoiler alert: this can be you!)

Who in your life would make it difficult?

What kind of art would you like to make if you could?

What if it wasn't called art?

What if it was just a hobby?

Are you good at any hobbies?

Could those results be considered art somehow?

Evaluate your present-day feelings about having more art exposure in your life right now using a scale of one to ten, where one is you need more convincing, and ten, you are ready to enjoy more art. Now evaluate:
Where are you?

If you are at a six right now, what would it take to get you to a ten?

What do you hope to gain as you begin to feel good about art again?

CHAPTER 7

THE ART MYTH

GAINING ART KNOWLEDGE, GOING TO THE RIGHT SCHOOLS, being naturally talented, and having a rich upbringing with lots of art exposure are all components of the theory that art is only for the elite few. Which means that it is not for the rest of us. The conclusion must be that we must 1) learn about art or 2) do without. Or we can buy into the Art Myth and try to become part of the Art Elite. I saw this latter option play out many times.

"I don't know anything about art, but I like what I know," became the new mantra for the elite. I learned that college students had a strong determination to learn all about art to justify their likes and dislikes regarding art so as not to ever be challenged. They were going to know about art so they could enjoy it. They could then defend their opinions to anyone, anytime. After all, they had a degree in the stuff! A sort of snobbism like this sprouts as a result of so much academic study of art. I have been around a lot of art snobs.

There are tons of books on how to understand art written by art educators, critics, and historians so the common folk can become part of the elite. Studying art is fun, but it is not necessary, as we have been discussing. Other authorities—colleges and other "higher learning"—can foster this myth with good intentions. Studying history is always a good thing. Understanding the elements of how a painting is put together adds another layer to our enjoyment if that's your thing. Again, it is fun, and I have done a lot of it. I have taught composition and design, art history, and art criticism as well. This book is not about that kind of activity. Allow your primal reactions to take first place; you can always study art later if that is your passion. I certainly loved it. But first, I listened to my gut! I suggest you do, too!

What is the alternative, do without art? What a shame! Here is the cost of that decision: people spending the entirety of their lives trying to show that they are worthy of their opinions about art. It's hard work. This effort is very much encouraged in our society. Not all societies in the world have the perceived requirement of needing to study before enjoying art.

By making art inaccessible, part of the richness of life is lost. It is somehow on the other side of that line in the sand. Tribal societies have no such restrictions. If they feel like tattooing or painting their bodies, they do. It is fascinating to see the magnificence of imagination when you view how many people incorporate art into their lives by decorating their bodies, their houses, and their surroundings. Why is art so compelling?

THE POWER OF ART

Art lifts us up! It is one thing to play all the notes on the page. It is another to make music! See, the thing is, your inner nature knows the difference between just playing notes and making music. We are not talking about technical prowess here. Many people are proficient technicians and are not really making art. True art speaks to our higher selves. Perhaps you could say there is a poet within all of us as well. Poetry is a way of naming words that convey the essential truth of things. Finding and portraying the essence of something can be done with other innovative methods, giving the audience a new way of seeing something. The message must ring a bell within us. Remember, art is communication. This inner knowing is not just a familiar recognition of a theme. When you have that "wow" sensation, it means the work has touched something profound in you. That lifts your spirits. It brings joy.

Sometimes, art is serendipitous. Artists often call this a "happy accident." That is, the artist did not really mean to put that trigger there, causing a great response. The trick for the artist, however, is to recognize when they have hit upon something that resonates in a profound way for the viewer. It calls for the artist to follow their own inner voice. The happy accident cannot be utilized if the artist doesn't see it as a way to bring the viewer the message. That is always the point. Communication. Unique expression that communicates.

What about chimpanzees and elephants who can swing paint around and splash up a work of art? Is that art? Is it valid art? Well, I would suggest maybe not to the chimp or the elephant but certainly to the viewer. It is like coming across a meadow flower, which is also a happy accident. It can still be a beautiful flower without the intention to startle you with beauty in that particular spot. See? The result and the way it communicates to you is what matters.

ELITISM AND ITS EFFECT

The Art Myth's rarefied air attracts people's natural ambitions to feel privileged, uncommon, and honored. People like exclusivity. They want to be in The Club.

We foster status in many ways, assuming it will enhance our lives. We drive a fancy car, buy a great house, show off our paycheck, brag about what we own, send our kids to private schools, and buy great art. Why? Are we afraid of our own common humanity? Do we just want status? Yes, most certainly.

I studied art because I loved it. No other reason. I had no goals. I just loved it. I followed my instincts, which led me toward it. College teaching led to me becoming an administrator of the Docent Program at the Toledo Museum of Art. *Docent* is another word for Museum Touring Guide. It is usually comprised of a group of volunteers who explain to those on the tour the attraction and meaning of artworks in the museum. I loved this job. I had a dedicated troop of affluent women volunteers to teach all of Toledo's youth about art. These volunteers were thirsty for all the art history I could pour into them. They were scratching an old itch that you, reader, may have too. They wanted to *know all* about art. Remember, they wanted to pick up where they left off.

And here is some good news:

ART KNOWLEDGE AND ART INSTINCTS CAN HAPPILY CO-EXIST

As I have said, just learning about art can be tremendous fun. I encourage all learning. Learning should be a lifelong pursuit. It has its own rewards. Everyone should keep growing.

Those interested women volunteers at the museum were strengthening their position in the community as experts. It was valuable to them as it increased their social status. The value of volunteering at a prestigious museum cannot be overstated. It promoted the Art Myth. What I saw, though, was that even after their education and training as docents, they still held the notion that they could not follow their intuition about art unless it fell into the parameters of the Art Myth. Mystifying.

What are the parameters of the Art Myth? Mostly, how does one recognize good art? Defensible art? What are the rules? Some reliable questions always arose: Is the artist respectable? How much did it cost? Is it famous enough? Does it go with the couch? Where did you buy this thing, anyway?

How much did you say it cost?

The Elitist Art Myth says it matters who made it, where, and how much it cost. The question, "Is the artist famous?" is a big one. Does it meet fashionable interior decorating standards? Are your friends going to laugh at you? These verify the mythical assumptions, such as street fairs are not as reliable a source for real art as a gallery or museum shop. I could make a long list of subjective rules that people think must be in place for art to be respected.

We at the museum worked on the docents' own art intuition after that. They began to realize that both notions about art, intellectual and intuitive, can coexist and enhance the whole art experience. One can know all about art and use art instincts at the same time. The docents became even more wonderful with the children, who were encouraged to just enjoy, react, and love what they were seeing. It was very rewarding. Everyone gained.

WHY CONFIDENCE IS IMPORTANT TO US

It is okay as well to admit that you do not know everything that is out there about anything. The experts can bring new ideas into play, and then you have a broader field from which to pick. That is a great way to use experts! Then *you* decide what you like best. And stick to it. The more you do this, the more you will regain your confidence. Renewing your confidence brings happiness, and happiness brings confidence. Confidence can be restored with practice. Yes. Only that. Give yourself the will for some practice trusting your own gut feeling, and give yourself some permission too. It is the best medicine. This book is intended to give you both—practice and permission. I can teach you some very easy ways to prove to yourself that you do react and that those reactions are trustworthy.

Reawakening your art instincts is a form of self-love. Not only will you be able to surround yourself with great art and art experiences but you will always feel more whole when you are able to trust yourself. It is key to our honesty with ourselves. When there is less self-loathing because we are mad at ourselves for not knowing more about art, life is simply better. We feel better about many things, as aesthetic judgments are required every day. It will be easier, with less strain and more fun! Fun is always a good thing.

REGAINING CONFIDENCE IN OUR JUDGMENT

Emotions versus intellect, feelings versus logic; here is what we know: Intellectual decisions are more indisputable. Facts are facts. How they are interpreted and utilized is another matter. That is what is disputable and variable—how facts are interpreted. We can see the logic of something and go against it any way we want for emotional reasons. It is debatable on a case-by-case basis about any topic.

In my opinion, it is not generally sensible to live with something you do not and maybe never did like. Liking something is enough reason to have it in your life.

I taught my son to say, "Because I don't want to," when being pressured to do something that he felt was against his better judgment. It is unarguable. What is a person supposed to say to convince you that your statement is wrong? It is the final argument.

Now, there are always folks who will try to convince you that you are wrong. Let them try. Maybe you will change your mind (and your feelings) about it. Or maybe you will confidently trust your own judgment.

I do think it is easier to change your thinking than your feelings. We often listen to debates in order to understand both sides of an argument. That's good. Gathering information when faced with a logical decision is a good thing and always valuable. After that, after you have heard all the intellectual reasons explaining why you should like or not like something, and you still like it, you should obey your instincts, in my view. Trust your gut! That's not a bad mantra.

CHAPTER 8

OUR ART ANGEL

THERE ARE TWO VOICES WE HEAR EVERY DAY. ANOTHER BENE-fit of living with your art instincts alive again is that you will tame the two voices you hear every time you encounter art. Let's look at the two voices talking to us every day—not just about art, but certainly about art!

Everyone acknowledges that we have opinionated inner voices that talk to us daily about everything. It's called self-talk. We all have the positive and the negative voices speaking to us all the time about everything. Self-talk is worth listening to, not just for opinions about our self-worth but also to remember we can be hard on ourselves, and we can also be encouraging to ourselves. Much is written about how to talk to yourself to reclaim self-esteem or how to avoid damaging children's self-esteem by teaching them to like themselves. Positive self-talk is a powerful tool.

What are you saying to yourself about art? Do you have some pet phrases you use when you encounter art? Some folks remind themselves that they really don't care about art. "It's not that important after all." Some people immediately bring to life old memories of when they tried their hardest and were humiliated or shamed for their apparent lack of good art judgment, as we acknowledged before. The words from our good art voices and our bad art voices can be brutally powerful.

List some of your pet phrases about art.

Let's examine the two voices we hear in our head every day about art and our relationship to them.

WHERE DID THE TWO VOICES COME FROM?
Mysterious, influential art voices are found everywhere. They are at school, in your neighbor's house, at the playground, and certainly from your parents. They travel with you everywhere, waiting for a chance to tell you what they think you MUST be told about you and art. They are ruthless in their attempts to convince you. They come from Art Judgment Land. What's that? A land with two landscapes. One is serene and lovely. The other is a land of strife and discomfort, where even trying to be better is discouraged.

The Art Angel who takes care of your Art Self is one character, and the Art Assassin is the art ninja who takes a karate chop to your art instincts every time you think positively about art. The two voices are at complete 180-degree odds. The conflict feels terrible to us. We want to believe the positive, but the negative is so seductive—and so commonly thought—we tend to buy it! That is generally true of all negativity, by the way. Think of how fast negative gossip travels compared to nice, positive, victorious stories. Positive things are just not as interesting. Think of how reading gossipy, juicy tidbits feeds our lower selves. Check out the news, and you will see what I mean. The negative travels further faster.

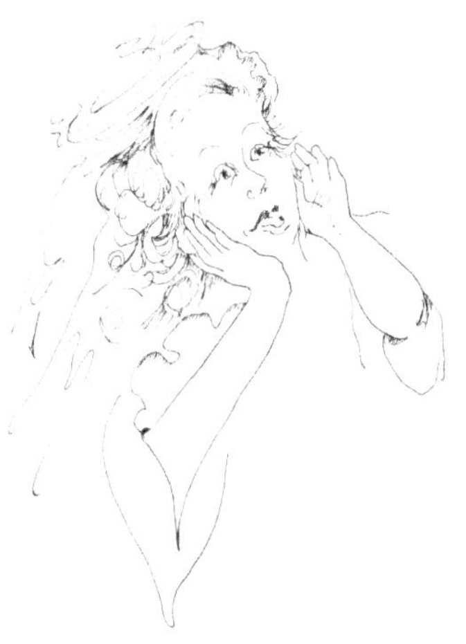

OUR ART ANGEL'S SWEET VOICE

The Art Angel lives in peace and serenity on the quiet end of Art Judgment Land. The colors of her life are light blue, with subtle pastel colors and white. Art Angel is like an art whisperer, soft-spoken and easily liked. She is always affirming how wonderful art is and calming down any negative self-talk you are engaging in. She is the image of light, hair flowing, halo, pointed toes, lyrical, and so appealing! She floats like a feather in the air, hands offering encouragement to you, with beautiful music playing, embellishing her words. Everything she says is hopeful, optimistic, and positive, and we love it! She never criticizes. She's sensitive and cares how you feel. She wants to make everything "all better"; she is nourishing your spirit all the time. Protecting your instincts is her positive mission. It works sometimes.

We want to believe her but feel unsure if she is actually right. It would sure be nice if she was right. We'd like to believe her and, thus, believe in ourselves.

THEN ART MISTAKES HAPPEN TO US

When the *art mistake* happens, children get that feeling that they are wrong, and they don't know why. The whole thing is confusing. It is a misunderstanding, but no one explains to the child that it wasn't actually a bad thing they did. Sometimes, the event is so minor no one even notices except the child. There's a nod of the head, rolled eyes, or a simple gesture that says they are not doing the right thing. The child simply feels bad and doesn't know why. The feeling is unmistakable. You remember such times, right?

Haven't you had something said to you that was another person's reaction to you, and you felt just awful? Maybe you didn't even know what they meant by what they said, but the feeling was plain. You did something wrong. They didn't like it. Remember how that feels?

You still remember, don't you?

See? It happens to adults too. As adults, we sometimes resolve it by believing that we were not destined to enjoy art anyway. We rationalize so the event has less importance or damage to our inner child. This is the event that the Art Angel is trying to prevent. She'd like to put a bandage on you so you will feel better than you do. Can you relate?

The trouble is we surrender to the other voice sometimes without even thinking about it. Negative reactions become automatic.

THE ART ASSASSIN TAKES OVER

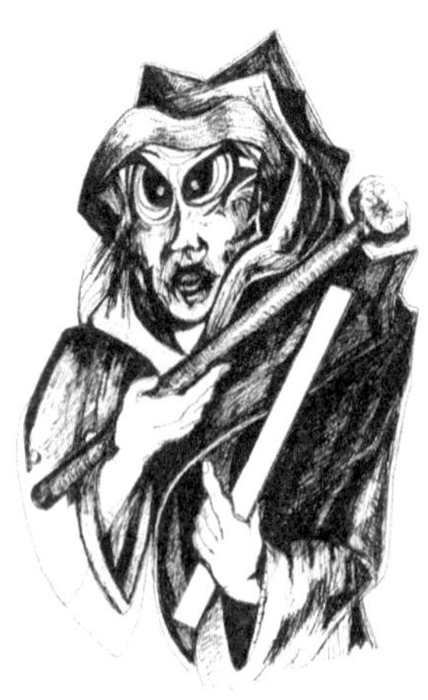

A second voice shows up. The Art Confidence Assassin is now in her glory. Time to strike! She's mean; she loves to pounce upon you while you are at your lowest, most doubtful place. Once the art mistake happens, it reaffirms what she has been saying all along—art is not for you.

She uses a karate chop to your brain. She carries an evil stick; she is very determined to strike you. She ruins every art experience, over and over. Glee is written all over her face as she seizes any opening to warn you that this art thing is not for you. "Don't even try it!" she warns. If you go ahead anyway, she blames you and fills you with guilt and grief. She always hammers the point home, over and over.

This voice is relentless in making you feel bad. It can keep you up at night with self-defensive arguments: "What was I thinking? I should have known better. You know, I thought I shouldn't buy that, do that, say that, etc." Familiar? Now she has you thinking the way she wants you to think.

Remember my story about street fairs and how people would judge my work? It was the Art Assassin's subtle temptation to listen to them. Turning my desire for approval of my artwork against me is a sly approach indeed. One has to be wary of the Art Assassin, who hides in all sorts of places, even at street fairs. She will do anything to get you to mistrust your judgment and assassinate your confidence in yourself, whether artist or art appreciator!

CLEVER GIRL! SHE GETS YOU WORKING AGAINST YOURSELF

She might tap you gently to remind you that you are clumsy when it comes to this art thing. Look out! The wand is ever ready to deliver a bigger blow to your confidence! When it comes to art, one stroke! Poof! There goes your art enjoyment!

Sometimes, she is unrecognizable, hiding in a friend's comment. She's sneaky too. She remembers everything! She keeps track to report back to you all the times you tried and failed at art—ruthless and relentless—so you can go back over your failures in art. Over and over. Her horrible intent is to kill all your art instincts so they never come back.

Has this ever happened to you? Of course it has, and not just about art. Does this sound familiar? You decide to buy a piece of jewelry, and that little voice starts to make you wonder if it is "just right." That's her! Making you wonder and mistrust your judgment.

Make a note about a time you remember changing your mind because you doubted your judgment.

The Art Angel is your only defense, your only ally. You may wonder, "Can I believe the Art Angel?" Her voice is not as strong as the Art Assassin's, and she's been proven wrong before. You waffle between the two voices and then just get tired of the struggle. "Forget it!"

It happens to all of us as children, and we live with the consequences for the rest of our lives. We then continue where the Art Assassin leaves off. We continue this internal self-talk battle. It's useful to remember when thinking about our confident childhood that we now carry on what well-meaning authorities (Art Assassins) started. We become harder on ourselves than they were.

IS THIS MAKING SENSE TO YOU? CAN YOU RELATE? Has it ever happened to you that you thought you could do something and found you might be wrong? You felt like you couldn't do it after all? Then, you proved your negative voice right! Note it.

What if it had gone the other way? What if, in fact, what you did was pretty good, but nobody praised you for it?

Can you see how the result might have been different?

Can you think of more examples?

Let's use our ever-ready "memory eraser." Let's wipe that look off their face; let's scrub the words they said from our memory. In fact, let's reverse what they said to us. Let's make this a positive image in the rearview mirror of our minds so that we can also get rid of the bad feelings we had because of them forever. Good! Now, doesn't that feel better? Give yourself a high five!

You are in control; you can change any thought at any time. You are not that hurt child anymore. You are an adult, and you understand why it happened. You also know that you need to feel better about it. So do it. Conjure up a resolution to that situation that leaves you feeling great.

CHAPTER 9

ART ARMOR

You were once a "Cute Art Kid." Cute Art Kids are those vulnerable, eager to learn, and respectful of authority. They are the kids who are most open prey to all influencers. We are talking about every kid who begins learning with a healthy appetite for all things positive. They are especially hungry for art when they are very young and innocent. They love life, they're full of confidence, and like we all once were, they are vulnerable.

Do you remember being like that?

Don't you agree that all little kids are cute? They are so sweet and open to possibilities that it makes it easy to forgive the Cute Art Kid for believing the adult authorities in life. How about if we forgave ourselves? We made some natural decisions, given what we were taught by people we respected. Forgiving ourselves for quitting on art is important if we are to make progress in enjoying art again. (You can declare it now if you are ready.)

Art mistakes happen to Cute Art Kids; they happened to all of us. Can you see why we might eventually give up on art? The Art Angel's daily positive statements were still outnumbered.

The Art Assassin won. The Art Assassin got in more blows than the Art Angel could counter. The art mistake inevitably happened to poor, innocent Cute Art Kid.

The Cute Art Kid is definitely in trouble and thoroughly confused; he thought he could do it. He must have been wrong. Again. He starts thinking the Art Assassin is right! He didn't expect the art mistake he encountered. He's even confused by his own reaction. The only human reaction to that emotion is to feel bad and become wary of doing it again.

ART ANGEL TRIES TO REPAIR THE DAMAGE

The weight of the job is too heavy. The Art Angel doesn't know how to do anything but be positive, but the job is too big. It is impossible to make a dent in the Cute Art Kid's mind now. The Art Assassin is winning yet again. In fact, she is taking over! Don't you wonder how many times the Cute Art Kid can take it?

For some people, it only takes one BIG bad art mistake to take them out. After all, we all have different tolerances for risk-taking. A really sensitive child may never put their toe in the water again if they felt a serious declaration was made that art is not for them. Others can take more bad experiences. Some just resist. Let's look at the ones who escape.

IS THE CUTE ART KID THE ONLY ONE
WHO'S HURTING?

As the Cute Art Kid looks around him, he sees that almost all the Art Kids have made art mistakes now. Most of the Art Kids are infected with self-doubt when it comes to art now. They worry about trying new things. Risk-taking, when it comes to art in general, seems like a bad idea now. Physically and emotionally, it is just too hard. Defensive behavior rises up. This seems funny because they never used to have to defend their art. "Mysterious art stuff" seems too hard for them now. It is somehow comforting to see that there are so many who feel this way. Cute Art Kid comes to terms with these new feelings about art.

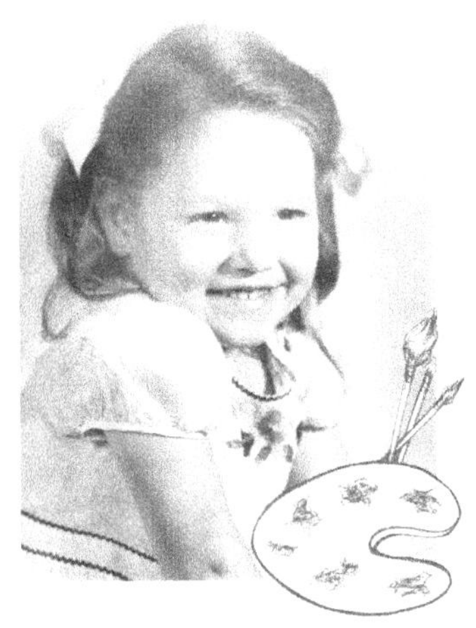

What is there to do when it comes to art in the future? All the wounded Art Kids conclude that it is best to just keep quiet, keep one's head down, and maybe no one will notice. They think, "At least being passed over, you don't have to explain that you are no longer sure of art and its place in your life. Just tell them you don't feel well—that should do it—just don't participate. Or maybe participate just enough to get along. That is the only thing that will feel good till this art boo-boo heals."

The problem is, however, that art wounds never completely heal without consciously addressing and erasing the event. Not healing the art boo-boos causes accumulated damage over a lifetime. From the trivial to the traumatic events, nothing gets left behind as we archive our emotional responses and come to more conclusive decisions. No wonder we reason that art is not for us. It is not evidential damage from only one event. Remember, our minds will look for evidence to prove a point. Once the premise is set ("Art is not for me!"), then we search for more proof. Of course, we find it. Plus, we allow others to deliver more evidence to us (people are only too happy to help you out with negativity), and we accept those conclusions too. More and more added evidence! That's the tragedy.

ARE ALL ART KIDS WOUNDED IN THE SAME WAY?

Art boo-boos are visible all over the place. There are more Art Kids who are affected by art mistakes now than those without art mistakes. Did some not feel the pain of those incidents? Do some not feel it? Really?

There are different sensitivity levels in different people. We are all alike and all different in our responses. One has to ask, do people really get over this? Even small wounds are still wounds. How are we taught to deal with pain? The pain of failure is serious, whether small or big, don't you think?

Wait! Some escaped the damage from their art mistakes? How did this happen?

There seem to be some Art Kids who are not infected. How can this be? If I feel so badly, why don't they? Who are these kids? And why did they not get infected with self-doubt? There is a small group of them. Yes! A select few known as the *Talenteds*. The Talenteds seem to have armor on that protects them from the Assassin! (Her spells don't work on them.) They keep doing things well and listening to the Art Angel instead of the Assassin. They created *art armor*, and now they are immune from art mistakes. Where do these Talenteds come from? Do you remember those guys?

Were you one of them for a while?

What happened?

THE TALENTEDS HAVE LEARNED A SECRET THAT PROTECTS THEM

The Talenteds have an inner confidence—it seems as if they always had it. We said at the beginning of our discussion that all little children feel remarkably confident. Otherwise, how would we ever learn to walk? Is that inner confidence the way they escaped the damage to their happy Art Self? Their art instinct was left intact as they did not doubt their abilities. They retained their art instincts and were happy to just love art because they like having fun! The idea of giving up fun was too strong. "One shouldn't have to give up fun," they think. They also recognize that everyone makes mistakes! They learn to still feel good when the art mistakes happen. They cope with failure. They don't always like every artistic thing they do, but they feel they have the right to do it, with a right or wrong result. This, again, is not a question for really small children to ponder. They feel entitled to fun. We should too if we can resist the urge to think we don't deserve it anymore because we are adults with responsibilities.

With a strong belief in themselves, the Talenteds do more and more art. The more art they do, the better they get at it. You can't practice something all the time and not get better at it. It's stopping the practice that does the harm. The Talenteds are undaunted. They believe they will eventually succeed. They see the mistakes as a way of learning what not to do and don't take it as personal failure. They seem unaffected by failure because the cost of not doing art again is too great to give.

They also think, "It's all so wonderful, doing this art thing. It's so fun; why would I give up fun?" No matter what the Art Assassin says, the Talenteds decide she could not possibly be talking to them. They are immune! They have art armor! Confidence!

IF CONFIDENCE IS ART ARMOR, HOW DO I GET SOME?
Wouldn't it be great to get some of that armor now? What if we got our confidence back when it comes to making and enjoying art? If it is just a matter of confidence, don't you agree it would be great? You could use it in other areas of your life too, right? A bonus by-product of regaining trust in your inner Art Self. We will be exploring ways to strengthen your art awareness, reawaken your instincts, and, thus, build your art confidence. This will naturally transfer to other parts of your life. Confidence is like that!

Where did this confident art armor come from? Was it always there? Some early influencers on this type of Art Kid protected their innate love of art with consistent praise and belief in the child. What a miracle praise can be! What happens if someone believes in you?

All little children think they can dance, sing, playact, paint, and draw; then the magic happens. They try to do it, and someone praises the effort! It's a win! It proves to them that the Art Angel was right! They listen to her more and more with every success. And then, more magic! Success becomes a habit. Others notice, and those Art Kids are singled out as Talenteds, and the art armor is formed and impenetrable. The Art Assassin doesn't have a chance with these kids ever again. It's just all so simple.

Really, is that all there is to it? Keeping confident in one's own efforts? Yes! It's the secret sauce of all happy lives. Confidence in our abilities makes us happy. And happiness makes us confident. Isn't that great? What a system!

Think now about a time when you felt supremely confident in something you did.

Did you ever do it again?

Would you do it now if you could?

Do you think you could if you tried?

It's hard to get rid of confidence if one has success because of it, don't you agree?

CHAPTER 10

GOOD NEWS! THE ART ANGEL NEVER GIVES UP ON US!

SHE SITS ON OUR SHOULDER ALL OUR LIVES. SHE'S STILL TRYing to say to you, "You can do it; believe me, you can do it!" Do you still hear her once in a while?

That may be why you picked up this book. That tiny, very indistinct voice is still trying to convince you that art in your life would be a good thing. Some of us listen later on into adulthood because we secretly think we might've been one of the Talenteds long ago. But it's never too late, right? If you have ever thought or seen evidence that maybe you are a Talented, I hope this book persuades you that it is not too late. Clearly, the Talenteds have joy from art in their lives because they are unafraid of art.

Then there are the Tryers. Some people figure out that we don't all have to be recognized as a Talented. Often, these people haven't simply tried and failed; they have tried and given up! We are all different in our sensitivity tolerance levels. Some people have to be hit hard to get them to see the point. The Art Assassin has her work cut out with them! Others are so sensitive that even a roll of the eyes or a frown will discourage them. You most likely know your level of sensitivity from other evidence in your life.

If you did try, and you surrendered for a time, you can still try again. Give yourself permission to do that. Take a class, watch an online video, visit a craft store. Remember, no rules; just dip your toe in the water at a comfortable pace. There is no reason to do without creating art in your life if you want to do that.

It may be that the joy of art is even greater after overcoming the Art Assassin's attempts at squelching art within you. Victory is sweet, and living well is the best revenge. Putting art back into one's life is living well. Opening the door to art allows us to enjoy the rich tapestry art can bring to life. Remember, art is everywhere for everyone. Isn't that reassuring? There are lots of opportunities to dabble in art. Think a moment about what art possibilities are in your town, neighborhood, club, church, school, and family. Just jot them down here so you can refer to them later.

MY OWN STORY AND HOW THE ART ANGEL WON

I want to tell you about my childhood because I was very lucky. You may be able to identify some things that didn't happen for you that could still happen with a few changes. I would like to point out events, people, and the environment that fostered my becoming an artist.

My childhood was an idyllic art environment. The Art Angel got a big boost of enthusiasm from my family.

All the adults around me thought I was a Talented, so I was! Self-fulfilling prophecy still works! I retained my childhood confidence, with lots of praise and validation for being creative.

I had a Huckleberry Finn childhood. Remember how creative he was? On his own, he solved problems as they came up and helped others do the same. We will see how problem-solving is an essential component of creativity. It keeps the imagination alive. Einstein was known to say that imagination is the greatest attribute of all. I tend to agree. It certainly is a muscle we want to begin to exercise again on our art journey.

My young creative life was a total art experience. As I said, I was allowed to be a confident problem-solver, which made all the difference. Of course, there were those mistakes, but deep down, my inner self knew I could do it. It's a tribute to my parents' faith in me. I feel sure that confidence can rarely be broken if thoroughly developed at a young age. Without any art lessons in my youth, I competed in college with accomplished artists through confidence. I believe I won because of the confidence of my childhood.

The sheer joy of making art was revered in my household. What a gift! We will be talking about how you can create an environment intentionally designed to promote creativity as a way of stimulating your own imagination and creative problem-solving. It will be fun!

CONFIDENCE AND FREEDOM

The single most important contributing factor to confidence building in my childhood was the extraordinary freedom I was allowed. Think back here to the amount of freedom you were allowed as a child.

Were there a lot of rules and regulations? Lots of guidelines, shoulds, and should nots?

Remember, you are an adult now and in charge of the rules in your life. What one rule given to you in childhood would you change if you could? (Any kind of rule can be listed here. "Don't make a mess," is a great example.)

You don't have to demolish your entire memory bank from childhood to release yourself from rules. Simply notice which rules do not serve you any longer, and write them down.

FREEDOM TO SOLVE PROBLEMS WAS THE GREAT GIFT
I was allowed to solve my own problems. I had a free and easy upbringing. I'm not fond of rules. Oh yes, I know society needs them. We have to remain safe, for instance. The main ingredient for my creative childhood was freedom. Freedom from rules. I think I don't like them because I didn't have any to restrict me. Now, I do not like restrictions, especially silly restrictions. I still do not walk down the middle of a road, but some rules are artificial and unnecessary. I had such amazing freedom because my folks trusted me to solve my own problems from early childhood. We do what is expected, don't we?
Think about your own expectations of yourself as you relate them to art right now, and make some notes.

It's painful when we feel we know something but are afraid to express it. Sometimes, we just know the right way, the answer, but fear it doesn't fit into the rules of others. Having to put those intuitions into constraints that limit how we think through a problem is a quiet consternation as we grow up. A mental straitjacket. I think it causes great internal frustration by stifling the creative process. To me, it proves how important it is to eliminate rules and give freedom of expression a chance to do its work.

Freedom enhances the ability to solve problems. Without the constraints of shoulds and should nots, cans and cannots, whys and why nots, we can dream up possibilities. You can see why not having any rules as a child was essential to my development as an artist. One simply must be free to make choices and design new solutions. That is the creative process. Solving any kind of problem creatively means imagining the end results and applying imagined processes to make it happen.

I was very lucky that all the reactions to my creative pursuits were met with encouragement. People around me understood that when trying to solve a problem, the first solution may not be the best solution. I was encouraged to try again or rethink the problem. What an amazing educational tool encouragement is. Therefore, I never felt any pain about the end results. There was always another try to be had, another solution to imagine. I was prevented from feeling inadequate or inconsequential because I was a child. They expected me to do my best, and I did, and I still do. That trust in my serious attempts prevented the pain of failure from settling into my being. I am grateful. It is part of my art armor.

MAIN STREET, MY HOME SWEET HOME

When I was eighteen months old, our house burned to the ground. We rented the only apartment there was in a nearby village. You know the Main Street block I lived on very well. You have seen villages like this one all over America. The entire commercial district was one block of two-story brick buildings. I lived over a store my entire childhood. It was great for any child with an imagination. You will see why in these next few pages.

MY STOREKEEPER FRIENDS CONTRIBUTED TO MY IMAGINATION

The stores were my playground growing up, and the clerks were my friends. There was a variety of personalities, both in the physical shops and the people who worked there. As I was a very extroverted youngster, I stopped in daily to chat with my adult friends. I learned retail! Always curious, I learned about the colors and textures in the downstairs dress shop. I was taught how to gift wrap by my gift store owner neighbor. All the ribbons and colors and paper a kid could want were on her counter. I loved it. It was a wondrous way to use one's imagination. Do you see that art is everywhere, and so are art teachers?

The hardware store was another abundant place full of everything you can imagine in little bins and nail kegs. It was one of my favorite haunts. Along with, of course, the dime store. It was a cornucopia of color and stuff, all cheap enough for me to actually buy. I still have an embroidered potholder I made when I was six from a kit I bought at the dime store. For a dime. I saved up.

THE DAWN THEATRE WAS SPOOKY AND GREAT!

The Dawn Theatre was an eerie and spooky place because I had to go upstairs to the projection room. I took my brother's supper up there to him when he was the projectionist. I had to go up narrow, tiny, winding, dark stairs to the small, dark room where film spools were spinning, strobing lights, blue, black,

and white images striking the
black walls. There was music, of
course, and dialogue all over the
place. It was magical, spooky, and
irresistible.

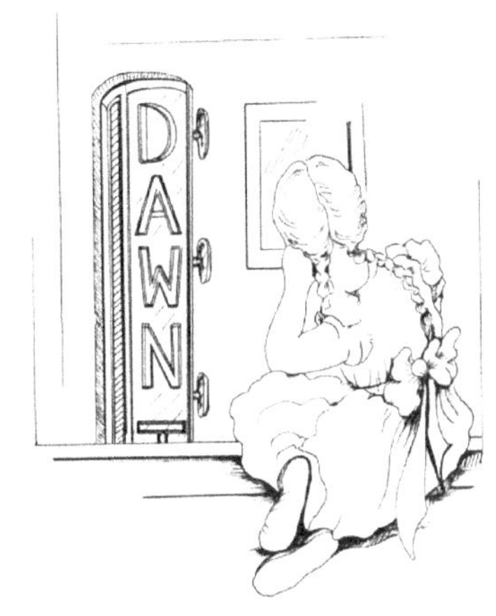

That projection room was on
the second floor, right across the
street from my bedroom. If my
brother left the theater window
open and I left my bedroom win-
dow open on my side of the street, I could watch movies! After
all, it cost seven cents to go the regular way. I saw all kinds of
movies through that window. There was no rating system, so
everything was open territory for my keen and interested eyes.
It was fascinating. More fodder for my growing imagination.

Can you think of places you used to go when you were a
child that were full of wonder?

Can you think of places that sparked your curiosity?

Can you think of places you remember with fondness because they were private places of fun (your best friend's place, your schoolyard, your grandparents' house)?

Try to recall a place that was your imagination's friendly place. You might have even had an imaginary friend, as many children do. That person is a comforting companion to whom we can express inner thoughts. Some places naturally foster that secret-garden type of comfort. Do you remember having such a private space for you and your imagination to reside?

CHAPTER 11

SOLVING PROBLEMS
MEANT DAILY FUN

MY BACKYARD ALLEY WAS FULL OF SENSATIONS. THE ALLEY was a dirt parking lot that supported the underside of the commercial stores I frequented daily. It, too, fascinated me. That's where the oil barrels that fueled the stores' stoves to warm everyone on those cold Michigan days were located. Oil-soaked ground was my playground. The roofs of the stores were tar-paper roofs, where we skipped along as if it weren't dangerous. I remember the smell of fresh tar on the hot summer days when they re-tarred those shabby roofs. Hot and black and smelly. We loved watching them make the roof all new again. I learned about regeneration with just a coat of something.

All of our senses were touched by our existence in that apartment. Keeping the senses alive is another way to sharpen your awareness so that when your instincts speak, you can hear them! What smells thrill you the most? Smells from the kitchen? Fresh linen? Leaves in the fall? New dandelions in spring? Damp moss?
Name some favorite smells.

We are beginning to bring new awareness to your art life with some basic noticing. I read once that artists are often more like hunters than farmers. Hunters have to notice every-thing in the forest, instantly, constantly aware, whereas you don't want those folks planting your corn! It's very likely not to be in straight rows. For that, you need the mentality that re-quires order and the sequential methods of the farmer. Artists use methods too, of course, but they are quite different. Staying keenly aware of bodily sensations and being sensitive to envi-ronmental conditions and other stimulation brings imagina-tion to the hunter (artist).

THE INCINERATOR WAS A TREASURE TROVE

Ahhhhh, the *incinerator*. A main feature in my young life. The incinerator was in the middle of the parking lot. It was a brick cubicle into which the stores put their trash to be burned. Noth-ing fancy—just a square brick wall around the dirt. It became a main imagination creator for me.

You should have seen what people threw away! The dentist threw stuff out there regularly, and we couldn't wait to discover it. I played with mercury often. It made a fascinating glob of shiny silver stuff that you could take to school, roll around in your hand to amaze your friends, and then pass around to the whole class! It is a wonder we weren't all poisoned! I played with false teeth, little vials of who-knows-what, other poisons, and pieces of tar into which the teeth were set when made. They looked like monster-mask-making material to me. Other plas-ter molds he threw out were like building blocks. It made for a great variety when we played store under the dining room table.

There was a little shelf under there where we used to dis-play our goods. The imagination that those forbidden substances provided for me was invaluable. The best art supplies ever—better than clay! However, we did have access to plenty of mud and clay down by the river. Clay was lame next to the stuff the dentist "gave" us.

The entire landscape of my childhood was an "art lab" with processes and products from my own hands and imagination. No restrictions were applied to the open turf for all my ideas. I was free to experiment with anything and everything. I found what worked and what did not. Remember, it is about failing sometimes as well. It was all fun, even though I was not always successful in completing an idea. I had done it. That is the point. I was free to do it.

MY FAMILY WERE GOOD PROBLEM SOLVERS

You may be thinking you did not have access to art materials or unlimited freedom. Very few do. I think I had an unusual advantage. I illustrate my childhood here for you to show you that 1) it can exist, and 2) it is beneficial to children's imaginations to let them try things. We had very little, of course. We had lost everything in the fire. My parents had six children and only this small apartment to make do. I never heard them complain.

We could always figure out a way to get something we wanted. It might not have been right away, and we might have had to make a plan. We had no money. Our revenue was innovation and a work ethic. We could make things; we could work and figure stuff out. That life had all the ingredients that make for creativity, freedom, no rules or judgments, curiosity, ingenuity, and problem-solving. Daily. These good values make for happy living. All of my siblings are creative and successful problem solvers.

TIME WAS ANOTHER GIFT I HAD

I will admit that life was much slower in my childhood days than now. I remember wondering in the fifties and sixties what people were going to do with all the free time that new dish-washing machines were going to give them. Now we hardly have time to load and unload it.

Consider your life and the time constraints on it. Everyone is too busy. Everyone has a full email inbox. Everyone needs a vacation. Everyone is worried about *STRESS!!!* (How stressful!) It's not a bad idea to slow life down sometimes. I have a dear friend who takes his watch off when he goes on vacation and over weekends. Ah, that old concept of freedom again. It even feels good to remove that watch. A sort of releasing ritual, isn't it?

With the unrelenting pressure of the smartphone by our side, giving everyone unlimited access to us, we are further and further away from lazy hours just to think, daydream, and create. Consider what time changes you might make.

I remember reading Maya Angelou, who reminded us that taking a day off is extremely valuable. I remember she liked to window shop. It is just a mindless thing to do: get a little walk in and let the mind roam. It's not a bad idea. How long has it been since you took such a walk? And just think, it's free! No rules, no restraints, just fun, right?

How can an artist freewheel ideas with restrictions placed on every move, every moment? It is essential that we have time to think. It is rumored that Picasso said artists should be subsidized to daydream! I don't doubt he said that. With open-ended days without TV in my early years, life was as entertaining as you could personally make it. There were no restrictions beyond one's own limited resources and imagination.

SHIRT CARDBOARDS WERE THE BEST!

My family loved that I could amuse myself with drawing and making things. Of course, there was no paper in the house because we didn't have any money. But my brother's job at Sears required him to wear a suit, shirt, and tie every day. He had his shirts laundered for that sharp, starched appearance, and they arrived neatly folded on a great piece of cardboard. Five or six a week! Shirt cardboards! Heaven. They were white on one side and gray on the other, with the quality and weight of poster board. Perfect for coloring!

I had a huge fan base in that little town. My family, of course, and beyond them, everyone in school, thought I was artistic. They thought I was talented, so I was! My piano teacher had me do drawings when I composed music to illustrate the songs. Thank goodness my mom saved them. Of course she did; I was the artist in the family.

CHILDREN ARE NATURALLY CREATIVE IF LEFT ALONE

As you can see, my own childhood was full of opportunities to be creative, for which I am grateful. When I learned through teaching that with small changes, one can change one's mindset about anything, I felt hopeful for those who were not as fortunate to have such encouragement as I had. Freedom is key to imaginative thinking. I had plenty of it.

The result today is that I now have an open-ended process when it comes to solving any problem creatively. It may be useful for you to read how I make a painting. It may shed some light on how it is to not have rules. Though I have an extensive education in art now, I use the same methods that caused me to have so much fun as a child.

Here's the thing, though: *you* also have freedom. Every day, you make choices about what to do with your time. I know, I know, you are busy. I would suggest there must be a moment or two a day that you could spend thinking creatively about something. It is easier to think life is in our way and that we are not in charge than to admit we can control some of it, at least. I think we can, even if it is only a moment or two a day.

I am reminded of Nelson Mandela, who was imprisoned for twenty-seven years and still managed to feel independent and free. You see, it is an inside job; no one has control of another's mind. Not even Mandela's jailers. He knew he was in control of his thoughts. If you accept this premise, you may find there is more room in your life than you thought for the art you used to love. It's worth exploring. Those moments you choose to be free will exercise that creative problem-solving muscle that is present within all of us. It's this very muscle I use every time I make a work of art.

ART IS SOLVING PROBLEMS!

THERE ARE ARTISTS WHO SET OUT TO DO A COMPLETED PAINTing and never vary from the initial blueprint or idea. I would suggest that the process of creative problem-solving also exists for that artist in the beginning sketches of the original idea.

I learned that, for me, it's best to start with an idea. I just do something based on getting that idea on canvas. I have solved the problem of getting started! And then, the painting takes over! Whatever that first blob of paint does, it now requires more problem-solving to get it to do what I want it to do . . . I am looking for a certain result and have to continually solve the new problems the painting presents because not all color is perfect, and not all strokes are perfect; it all needs constant correction. I love that. To me, that is the fun. I am not interested in just filling in the blanks. I love the challenge when the paint doesn't flow correctly, or the brush is wrong, and I have to change paths.

Have you ever heard the phrase "necessity is the mother of invention"? It's so true. I see the old path won't work because it took a ninety-degree turn somewhere, and now I have to resolve that new issue to get the desired result.

I am able to sell my work because I no longer care about the finished result. If I thought someone was taking away the process, I would go kicking and screaming! The process of painting, solving all those visual problems, is what is fun to me. It is wonderful to see one of my paintings bring joy to someone.

I believe someone once asked Picasso which was his favorite painting, and he reportedly said, "The next one!" I get it. It's the process and not the product that intrigues me.

DO YOU STILL FIND THE ARTWORK INTERESTING? THE BEST TEST!

My method of painting doesn't make for boring paintings! They are not static; they show the path the painting took to become. I was once taught to show "the evidence of the struggle." To me, it is a lovely thing to see the path unfold.

Painting was refined in the sixteenth century, beyond which most artists could never achieve better. It's logical when you consider that there would have to come a time when humans could not paint any better than what has been done. There are variations and innovations and new materials and methods, of course, but as far as creating better paintings than what was done in the Renaissance? It probably won't happen.

It's lovely to look at great paintings, and it's great to own them, of course. One measure of a great painting you can use is to keep asking, "Is it still interesting?" That is a good test. If it is boring, get rid of it. I don't care if it is considered a masterpiece. It must remain interesting to you to satisfy that inner child instinct we have been discussing. I like those paintings where I see something different all the time. They remain interesting to me, and I want to continue to engage with them.

My own objective in my paintings is to give my audience as much information as they need to rough out the idea and then let them bring what they have to the art experience. I believe it's more satisfying for everyone that way. This is consistent with my belief that art is a two-way communication. If I continually receive the same message from a work of art, doesn't it follow that I might become bored? Overly familiar with it? With nothing more to learn?

For my part in making art, I am not interested in making maps of faces, rooms, or landscapes. I do not want to follow a formula every time. If it is boring to make, it *has* to be boring to view. I want to suggest the essence of something, give it an atmosphere, and let the viewer fill in the blanks. That's interesting!

FREEDOM MADE ALL THE DIFFERENCE FOR ME

My mother was especially great at providing freedom. She thought it was natural to feel free. She once told me that she thought children just grew up; it never occurred to her to micromanage our daily lives. She provided a warm and loving environment when we got home, but our day outside of the house was our day. She trusted us to solve our own problems and be smart. Hurray for me! Lucky again . . . What an advantage for an imaginative child!

Freedom is THE great advantage for imagination. Remember, I think all children are imaginative. Their imaginations need feeding on a consistent basis. There have been studies done on what reading fairy tales does for children, read *The Uses of Enchantment* by Bruce Bettelheim. His book is listed with other titles of additional reading at the back of this book for those who want to explore related ideas further. Bettelheim's studies suggest that children have an inner life wherein they know their own problems. The reading of fairy tales, reading many of them and many times, Bettelheim further suggests, will provide a child with fantasy characters who solve the problems the child reading the story is facing. It is then simple for the child to see how problems are solved. The child learns there is good and evil in the world and that it feels good to be victorious, ally with the good guy, and be rescued. The point is that reading fairytales comforts the child while providing solutions. I read many of them! In today's world, video games may be offering some similarly analogous stories for players.

OUR HOME WAS FULL OF RESOURCES—NOT!

My mother's house was full of resources as I lived in an era when things were made from scratch (code for "made from whatever there is around the house and not necessarily always the right ingredient"). It made for some interesting results. The freedom and trust she placed in me can be seen in this little story of when I was six years old. I told her I was bored. It was summer, and I had nothing to do. I was in the kitchen, and she said, "Here! Paint that cupboard." She handed me a gallon of paint (no newspapers, since we didn't have any) and a brush, and I painted the cupboard. What a sense of trust she placed in me! What a confidence builder! We sometimes handle children with kid gloves when they are much more able than we think. She didn't give me a toy. She gave me a grown-up job! Lucky me. I rose to the occasion. Imagine the gift of confidence she gave me.

HOW ARE YOUR PROBLEM-SOLVING SKILLS DOING RIGHT NOW?

Remember, we know that problem-solving is an essential ingredient of creativity. In becoming art aware, we want to check our current problem-solving skills.

Here, solve this problem. You need something over the couch, something decorative to enhance the space. What?

Write out your initial answer. Don't think. Just react.

What's the first criteria (size, color, mood, message, anything else?)?

Where could you find a piece that suits you (online, locally)?

How much do you want to spend?

Could you find the money if you found a piece that is just right but beyond your present budget?

Is there someone whom you could consult for options?

What's the timeline? Now? Do you need to save up for it? Is it in the future? If so, when?

Ask yourself, "Shall I keep what's there? Why or why not?"

Do someone else's feelings need to be considered? Are you free to decide to do whatever you want? Can you change that?

Do you need a new sofa? Maybe that is the problem. Maybe you need to look at the whole room and how everything fits in. What do you consider? And why? That is the process. Once you have some answers and define what you DO NOT WANT, you can decide what you DO WANT. Tip: refine a system you can rely upon when making such a decision. Physical considerations like size, color, mood, and message are all useful determinants. And, of course, the ever-important question when you see it: do I like it? (Spoiler alert: a mirror is a safe solution).

Giving yourself creative options is essential. You must feel free to solve the problem. Maria Montessori, the great educator, understood and believed that if you gave children respect and a task, they would do it. That gave children permission to succeed and benefit greatly from their efforts. Might they fail? Yes, they might. Isn't there value to having been given the trust to do something, even if it wasn't entirely successful? Success also comes from trying. Allowing a child to figure stuff out is a great gift. Isn't that what we want as parents and teachers? A child who grows up to be an independent and critical thinker? Everyone benefits from a society where people feel capable. It's always better to feel like a winner. How can you if you are never given anything of value to prove to yourself that you can do it?

CHAPTER 13

THE MOTT MISSION MEANT MORE ART!

IN FLINT, MICHIGAN, THE MOTT FOUNDATION WAS ESTAB-lished by the Motts of the well-known apple empire. Recognize Mott's applesauce? The Mott Foundation was established to benefit the Flint area with educational programs. Flint Community College, now the Mott Community College, and adult extension courses are still funded by the Mott Foundation bequest after more than fifty years. What a gift! For underprivileged kids, it was a huge advantage. I was one.

My mother was an undaunted, curious learner all her life. Every year, she would take another Mott Foundation course, and we would learn too (especially me). We couldn't wait for the next round of interesting projects each winter. The house would turn upside down for it.

There was the year we braided rugs and cut up every old piece of clothing in the house, which we four-braided into strips that we sewed together into rugs that lasted thirty years—another real accomplishment from a child's point of view. Useful, real rugs that we had made ourselves. It was grown-up work.

We once made hair ornaments out of the scrap leather the shoe repair man threw away after trimming shoe soles. Fantastic, beautiful leather hair ornaments.

I can still see Mom's little four-foot, eleven-inch frame upholstering a big couch. Thank you, Mott Foundation. And Mom.

There are resources everywhere if you look for them. Find a place where you might expand your curiosity and skills. Solve new problems! Expanding life has great rewards beyond the adventure itself. Find yourself a Mott Foundation or natural resource. Are there some courses right around you now that you could take? (Very little risk for a possibly great reward. Just sayin'!)

Take a minute and jot down some of the nearby resources you could visit.

Could you drop in again? Would you? Why or why not?

What's their schedule?

What's their cost?

WE DIDN'T JUST BRAID RUGS

One Christmas, everyone in the family got carved leather billfolds and purses. The "millinery" year was a favorite of mine. First of all, it's a great word. Second, millinery supply houses are amazing color and texture training places for a young art-minded kid. Felt was steamed over a wooden head block to make a hat. Feathers were evidence of exotic birds somewhere.

Netting (as was the style back then) was fantastic as we made our Easter bonnets that year, and we felt like Hollywood stars. Our hats were *great.* Think of the originality of taking a piece of felt and steaming it over a head-shaped block of wood to make it into a hat. Magic! It was so fun! I was a very stylish twelve-year-old.

My mother was gifted with her hands; she could sew, knit, or crochet anything. She taught me to knit when I was four. When I asked her why, she said, "You wouldn't leave me alone!" I remember why. I saw the joy on her face when she spent any extra time happily knitting us sweaters, socks, mittens, and hats. I wanted to do that too. Don't you remember the joy you can feel when you have made something that makes you proud? Write down a memory of something you once made that made you proud.

CREATIVITY WAS A SURVIVAL MECHANISM

My mother lost her mother when she was six and was fostered by Victorian ladies who really didn't like children. She learned quickly to be self-contained and quiet. She remained that way all her life. That internal life she created included the satisfaction from what she could do alone, by herself. She was quarantined when she was nine and learned intricate crochet, which most adults cannot do today. I have examples of the lace she made for pillowcases and towels. She was a great survivor of her loneliness because she was creative. She regarded creativity as a sanctuary for the soul. She worked hard all day so she could be creative in the leftover hours. All of her children took pride in their work, knowing the main thing was to feel productive. If one could make work into play, we did it. And so did she.

See! No rules—no authority said she couldn't do this, so she could! Can you see how if you give yourself permission to try something creative, you might actually like it and do it well? The two things go together, of course; being creative is a joyful activity. If it is simply working with a new tool in the kitchen or garage, it can bring very meaningful joy to your life.
Does this remind you of anything you used to think you might like to do someday?

ADVERSITY AS AN ADVANTAGE

Part of the reason we never had any resources is because, when I was a baby, our house burned to the ground. We moved to a nearby village into the only apartment that was available. It was a railroad-style string of rooms over a store downtown. From then on, I lived on Main Street, USA. The first room hovered over the main street of the village. You know the row of two-story brick buildings that make up the entire one-block town. They are universally seen all over the nation. I had a fantastic look at that world from my bedroom window. It was more imagination-building material handed to me through adversity. Because we had lost everything, it caused us to solve problems out of necessity every day. One must do that when starting from zero.

Except for one pair of light-blue birthday shorts I received when I was twelve, I never had any store-bought clothes until I was grown up! I didn't know clothes were designed to be one-size-fits-all in stores (they are basically "one-fits-no-one" sizes). We tailored everything to our own likes and shapes. The reason we made all of our clothes was, of course, because it was cheaper, and the results again became art. We expressed individualism every time we made something because it was way more fun than following the rules. The results were spectacular, and they always fit me! We made our own patterns too. Why not? Another great benefit: fashion design! We did not have hot water in that apartment, but we did have a great sewing machine. My mother's priorities seem now to me to have been in the right order. Lucky me, again.

NONE GREATER THAN MY ART-ENHANCING CHILDHOOD

There were no art classes in that little rural village, but it didn't matter since my life was like an art lab. I'm suggesting here that you can create a mental atmosphere that will let you enjoy art without art classes too.

The greatest benefit to not having an art teacher is that I might have actually been saved from some early rules about how art is supposed to be. I had no expectations to inhibit my imagination. I was spared the "SHOULDS" about art.

Educators can often restrict ideas with rules instead of expanding ideas. Art education with its various effects can sometimes have unintended consequences. Teachers are all very different, but they often want to be right; they are *the teachers*, after all. You, the student, are required to respect that. I was spared rules because I had no art education. Instead, I had the wonder of fabrics and lots of open time to explore the world. Is it any wonder I have been an artist all my life? I couldn't help it. I became a teacher to share all the wonders of art with as many as would listen.

I do have other acquired skills. But it's the small village confidence that resides within me that allows me to know I can accomplish things outside of my own experience. I'm telling you that you can create a mental attitude toward art that will be satisfying without sacrificing who you are for the rest of your life. Art can live alongside whatever else you do in life. Art is a very amiable partner. There is no conflict between it and anything else. That is the beauty of art. It is everywhere, all the time, for everyone to enjoy. No conflict. Just enrichment for your life. That's worth pursuing, right?

CHAPTER 14

FREEDOM AND ART

GOETHE IS SOMETIMES CREDITED WITH SAYING THAT BOLD-
ness has genius in it. I have heard this attributed to others as
well. Whoever said it knew the score. Do the thing, and get the
power is another oft-quoted way of saying the same thing.

This is an especially important message to you, my dear
reader. It is easy to shy away from what we perceive to be bold.
We are actually taught to be a little more reserved. In my own
childhood, I remember people telling me to dream less big, be
a little quieter about my opinions, hold it down, and tone it
down. Thank goodness for my stubborn self! I just couldn't do
that. I knew I had something to say.

At home, my opinions were valued as contributions from
a child to the family discussion. I thought that would work in
the outer world, though we know it doesn't always. In fact, it
threatens some people who like to keep the status quo.

I really think that the family is the most influential factor
in growing up. If your family believes in you, you have it made!
If not, people naturally search for that mentor, that influence
in life that can point out a different way. Again, thank goodness
for positive influencers. Here's to all those who generously encourage children to be their best, bold selves.

Picasso invented cubism! Talk about bold! To the aver-
age person, a Cubist portrait is not only unrecognizable as a
human face, but some even find it repugnant. The paintings
are uncomfortable for many. People generally prefer realistic,

beautiful renderings of the human face. Picasso supposedly said, "When you lie on the bed and close one eye, you see something. If you close that eye and open the other, the view is different. In cubism, I painted both views." Now that is interesting. Very innovative. Artists began looking for other ways to present artistic interpretations of life.

The most important thing is to "just do it." Giving yourself permission to do it badly is a good first step. If you are the only one it must please, then everything is okay all the time. Right? When it feels wrong to you, change it. You will find that just doing it has genius in it. You may surprise yourself. Allow serendipity to be your partner, take chances, and just do it. Listen to Yoda, who said something like, "There is no trying; there is only doing." I also say give yourself points for *trying*; it is a form of doing.

Picasso also reportedly said, "Don't become an artist unless you have to." Well, as you can imagine, I had to. I write a lot about Picasso because he was on the movie theater newsreel often. He was famous, aging, and still charismatic. He made the artist's life look wonderful. I don't remember a single other real artist influence in my childhood. Lucky me. No rules about art. No expectations. It was just there for me to explore on my own.

As a child, when I saw Picasso and his fame, I thought my own name, Seirmarco, was just like the name Picasso. It had the same ring to it, I thought. I could see fame and fortune in my future. You will not find any paintings out there with my full name, Louise Seirmarco-Yale. I chose to honor my family name and produce famous *Seirmarco* paintings.

I chose the artist's path because it was so strong within me. I realize now that just because it is not always expressed openly as it was in my case, it is often strong within others. They just don't show it. I didn't know I was being bold.

Let me add here that it takes boldness to change your mind and opinions about something as you are doing now. It's great that you feel drawn strongly enough to take bold steps in going in a new direction. Congratulations. Boldness has genius in it.

HOW MUCH FREEDOM CAN WE GIVE CHILDREN?

I want to speak again about freedom in children's lives being essential to their trusting their instincts and judgments. It's important to help your own child feel free. I am not talking about letting your children roam about with no concerns for safety. As you read about my very free childhood, which I feel helped my creative problem-solving, I will remind you that those were different times. I am very aware of how afraid today's parents have become, for good reason. It is a different world, for sure. My childhood in the 1940s and 1950s in America felt safe and secure. I once arrived home to my father saying to me, "You don't stop at stop signs on your bike?" Someone had called him. I hadn't stopped. If it's true that it "takes a village" to raise a child, I was certainly lucky to have been in such a village.

I want to make a point here, however, that all children through the ages have had dangers from which they had to be kept safe. The world is a dangerous place. We had no seat belts; cars were less safe in general. My friend ran over his wife because there was no seat belt on her when he had a fender bender; the door flew open, she fell out, and he ran over her. (I have worn a seat belt every day since.) Accidents always happen. Kidnapping did occur. Ever-present bullying is an age-old strategy that always preyed upon weaker subjects. With the freedom children had to roam about the woods or play in a stream, it seems to me the dangers were then about the same as they are now for such adventures.

Rural American children faced dangers on the farm, using dangerous equipment. I knew a girl who got her arm caught in the wringer-style washing machine that we used then. We played with knives, hatchets, and other grown-up tools that were dangerous too. Our parents were preparing us for adulthood, which required the use of such tools.

The dangers then were more obvious. Today's children sit in front of social media and TV without regard to another danger: what is being taught to them. Life is insidiously dangerous in ways we don't even know yet. Even schools are dangerous. So perhaps the question is not about whether or not danger is present.

DANGER SEEMS WORSE TODAY

There is more news available about what can happen to a kid. Today, we have social media and news media spreading much more communication about the negative aspects of life. Twenty-four hours a day, we hear about tragedy. That was not always the case; we were less fearful, perhaps because we were less informed daily of terrible events. There are more guns now and more protests all over the media, not just in the local newspapers as in the days of old. With so much more exposure to negative news, it has to be concluded that it *seems* like there are more dangers. And maybe there are. So, what's a mother to do?

Naturally, parents are worried. Here, I am not addressing the parent who is sensibly cautious about their child's physical safety. I am talking about hovering over a child's every move and micromanaging every mood, thought, and statement. That child is never able to express an opinion without judgment.

I know such parents who are so concerned that the child be proper, well-mannered, of course, accomplished, well-dressed, and well-behaved that the child's own desires are smothered. This does not seem healthy to me for many reasons. For our purposes here, I believe it makes a child feel they can't be trusted. Clearly, the parents' message to that child is, "Check with me first to make sure you are doing (thinking, acting, looking) right." In my opinion, there go any natural instincts that child has to express himself through art. Rules. Rules. Rules. We are not born with them.

THE SOLUTION IS FREEDOM WITH A FENCE AROUND IT
The answer is freedom with a fence around it. One cannot let a little child roam the streets freely today. Certainly, though, there must be a safe place for that child to roam. I was once criticized for letting my son buy his own Happy Meal. He was five years old. I gave him money and sent him to the counter with the words to say and how it should go. I was no more than twenty feet away. I was vigilant, to say the least. He came back all puffed up and proud that he had done that grown-up thing. Freedom with a fence around it was my answer. I was his safety net; he knew it, and I knew it, and he's a very critical thinker today.

I once read a story about two boys. They were walking when a car pulled up to them, and the driver said to them, "Your mother sent me to get you." One boy got in the car, and the other did not. When asked why he did not get in the car, the safe boy said, "I just didn't think my mother would send a stranger to get me." See? He was a critical thinker. The other boy did what he was told without questioning it. In parenting, we must decide which battle to fight so we don't lose the war.

Actually, children like guidelines. It is awful, even as an adult, to live in flux, never knowing the way to please or get ahead or get approval. The concept of freedom with a fence around it gives us all some boundaries within which the imagination can soar. The concept that all is okay as long as one doesn't go beyond the boundary is secure and comforting.

When I taught art to school children, we had some social guidelines within the art room. Clean up after yourself. Don't touch another person's artwork. Be kind. Keep to your own space. Don't bother your neighbor. You get the idea. Freedom to create was foremost, with some rules that didn't allow anyone to impinge on another's creativity. It worked well because the children knew how far they could go. They actually liked being respected, too, so they could also do their best. Freedom with a fence around it. It works.

Once children feel free and secure at the same time, they explore with unbridled enthusiasm. The results that come about reinforce their art armor (confidence), and of course, their instincts strengthen with each success.

PARENTING ART KIDS

Sometimes, it is really obvious that a child is gifted; some children seem gifted artistically (or mathematically, or musically; you get the point). So, what can a parent do to not mess that up? Our premise here has been that well-meaning adults *can* mess up a child's understanding of himself. It should be of serious concern to any parent.

Gifted children are special-needs kids too. They are highly sensitive and prone to what is known as impostor syndrome. That means they feel someone will find out that what they are known to be good at comes so easily to them that certainly it cannot be that special. It's a real thing. They feel they are misleading others into believing they are more talented than they themselves actually think they are. They are afraid of being found out.

This, of course, is a false notion. We all recognize a musical prodigy, for instance. In accordance with our premise here, fostering the talents of a potentially gifted child does not have to mean more lessons, more expectations, and more rules to live by for that child. I know children who stay up until one in the morning doing homework because they are expected to be high achievers. Seems like a childhood lost to me. Now, if they love it, that is different, as the internal motivation is to pursue what makes them happy, not just achievement.

I have found that parents who think they have a talented child are not sure what they should do about it. It brings out the art insecurities of the adults. Quite often, they do not think of themselves as artistic, and yet they have a child who seems artistic. "How did this happen?" they think. Then, someone brings up the fact that a relative on one side or another was an artist. "Ahhh . . ." they think, "it must be in the DNA."

This reasoning helps parents because they are also not sure the person (usually a teacher) who reported this above-average creative activity can be trusted. If not, maybe they shouldn't try to turn their daily lives upside down to accommodate this newfound talent.

What they really want is to do well by their child. Obviously. Doesn't every parent want the best for their child? What if the child's talent is extraordinary? One would like to encourage an unusually talented child, right? "What if this child could be famous someday? I have to help them . . . it's only fair."

But how?

"I don't know anything about art to help them realize their potential," they think. In any new endeavor or area of knowledge, we don't know what we don't know. Art is new territory for the art-insecure parents. What are the questions to ask? Who would we even ask? Parents think the problem is finding *who* can guide them. *Who* can help their children fulfill any art potential they may have? *Where* are these people who know about talented Art Kids?

Parents begin a search for the perfect teacher (private lessons), a role model (working artist), or an art learning situation (art camps, an art course). They worry about the logistics of the right art exposure for their kid. Now new questions begin to arise. "How does one know what is the right art exposure for an artistic child? Should we be going to museums? And what do we do when we get there? How much is this going to cost? Can we do this for our child right now? Right here? Where we live?"

Much of this evaluation is correct thinking, which usually results in great art adventures for the child. Even without a strategy, some of it is very successful. There is also an added benefit that the whole family gets more art exposure—definitely positive and enjoyable experiences for everyone.

Is it enough? Can it be the wrong kind of exposure for this specific kid? Parents can spend a lot of time, energy, and money providing what they hope is a productive art experience for their children. Keeping the objective of fulfilling the child's potential in mind is a good guide. The real issue is how to protect and grow a child's art interest, divergent thinking, and curiosity without damaging it in the process. This must be a consideration.

What parents need to do, mostly, is to use their strong parental voice to encourage their children, no matter what talents appear. Wouldn't you agree this is essential? This is true for parents of children with exceptional athletic ability. Certainly, parenting an obviously musical child takes lots of parental support. Mathematical children, children who show leadership, or good readers—all need to soar with their strengths. Any observant parent can spot their child's strengths. Sometimes, however, the emphasis goes to their weaknesses, the rationale being that the strengths are already there and don't need strengthening further. It is our strengths that make us successful. It is always more rewarding to do what we do best. Parents who can see that can support their children by offering opportunities to strengthen their strengths.

The parental voice is one of the strongest influences in our lives. Our self-talk as adults often reflects and uses phrases we were told about ourselves by a parent. We must believe and trust our parents, who are in charge of our safety when we are young and vulnerable. What parents say matters! Whether what they say is true or not.

The most important gift a parent can give a child is a strong sense of self-worth. Self-esteem and confidence arm us to walk through life successfully and happily. We must like ourselves and feel valuable.

Parents often detect obviously art-interested young children. They are not surprised when another adult sees that same drive. Knowing the child loves art should make it easy to praise any imaginative thing they do as brilliant and wonderful.

Parents who guide their children in all aspects of life, showing them what to do as examples of doing it "right," may do a disservice to the Art Kid. Children are not adults. When adults correct a drawing or show them how something should look, giving examples and rules about creating a work of art, they limit a child's creative thinking. Even coloring books point out to a child how something is supposed to look. And their drawings don't look like that. Children see differently, and that's the beauty of it all.

It is not the parent's job to criticize or suggest, even when they think it is constructive. This author is not sure there *is* such a thing as constructive criticism. The implied message is always, "You could have done better." That is discouraging to everyone. Criticizing a child's work always reminds the child of what is lacking. If the parent's objective is to support the child's talent, then why not let them know how great they are so they will keep doing it? It's fairly easy to have praising phrases at the ready!

It is possible to urge the child to think differently about the work without dictating how it could be better. How does one do this? By asking questions. Children can change their minds about what they want to express better than well-meaning adults can presume. Parents often want to change it to be done their way, the adult way, the right way. Huh?

What kind of questions could one ask of a child to get them to explore new ways to express their message without hurting their creativity? "Can you tell me a story about this drawing?" pulls out of the child's imagination the circumstances of the drawing. The child can decide whether the drawing does or doesn't convey what he or she meant to say. Then, any change in the drawing is productive and feels good to the child. Only when the child's thinking changes can the drawing be improved in a way that doesn't harm the child's creativity.

Some parents view their children as extensions of themselves. Hovering over every move the child makes lest it reflect badly on the parents is very limiting to creativity. Remembering that each of us is unique could guide parents into letting their children find the best path to their own greatness. "Let them lead, then you follow" is a good mantra. Feed their curiosity. Let them react.

It is also common for parents to see a child as a personal project. Naturally, they do not want to fail as parents. They want to produce the perfect product. When challenged by a child who is already better at something than they will ever be, it is difficult to just be an observer.

Pursuing art can be threatening to a parent who sees the artist's life as a whimsical, frivolous, indulgent life. Artists have been portrayed as irresponsible, eccentric, even crazy misfits in society who will never get a "real" job or be able to make a living, and that scares parents. All of us want to produce productive, happy futures for our children. Indulging in something as fun as art seems to be too indulgent. Too carefree. One must be serious! And work hard—even at stuff they don't like—for years to be successful is a common thread in society's message.

It's okay for art to be a hobby. That rationalizes and neutralizes parents' fear. Parents who constantly remind a growing creative art mind that there are more serious endeavors available send an enduring and subtle negative message.

The answer? Let art be fun! Always fun! Worthy of praise! Messages of value and worth! Enigmatic answers are best. Children do not need detailed analysis and reports on their work. Just the look of appreciation in a parent's eyes is all that is required.

"That's great!" "Wow!" "I love it!" "Keep going!" "You're so good at this!"

And if the picture is really incomplete or puzzling, ask the famous question, "Can you tell me about this? What is the story here?" Your child will be happy to tell you *all* about it. Then you can say, *"That's great!!"* See?

It is good advice to let the child lead, and you follow. We don't know the future or where the child is headed. It stands to reason then, that we can't give good advice with certainty. We can keep them safe with rules about crossing the street, but this is different. They know what is good for them. It will all make sense later. Let them go. Let them proceed. Let them find their own creative way.

A parent's voice is the strongest voice of all in a child's life. As I have attempted to show, many a thoughtless comment has destroyed a kid's hopes. Let them feel joy in what they do, and you will feel it too. Art is good for all children everywhere, all the time. We know that play is extremely valuable to children. It is how we learn. When is that child supposed to feel free if not during play? My suggestion here is that the only thing that child needs is love and support and lots of praise. Doing what is fun is also productive, especially in building art confidence.

Remember, children are not living in our time. Their childhood cannot, by nature, use the same information that informed our childhood. So, keep it to yourself. Nostalgic stories are one thing, and they are valuable, but passing along rules for living a life you cannot live is another. Present-day adventures inform and prepare them for their future. Give them opportunities. Give them praise. The rewards of parental encouragement cannot be overestimated.

You will be rewarded one day when you watch your child fulfill his creative potential, and you will know they did it by themselves, which has its own intrinsic reward.

So, buy some art supplies; let the child make a mess and

take pride in cleaning their own brushes. Make a place for art in your household's daily life as a comfortable partner in protecting and growing your child's talents. You will be glad you did. Think of freedom with a fence around it. Your child will be able to explore imaginative ideas. In the future, you will have the satisfying result of a happy child, the reward for the big job of having parented a talented kid well.

It's worth it.

I didn't say it is easy. Changing thinking is challenging. Thank you for your interest in being a better parent on a different level. Art needs your child, and your child needs art. Life is full of risks. And so is art. Just be bold.

CHAPTER 15

ART RISKS

DEAR READER AND RECOVERING ART LOVER, WHAT IS THE RISK of making a bad art choice? Let's examine how bad the results of a poor art decision could be.

The risk might be that the drapes might be wrong. (According to whom?) Or that your neighbors will laugh at the price you paid. (Don't tell them!) Or that you might have to explain WHY you like what you chose. (You could say, "I don't know. I just liked it!")

As I've mentioned before, I taught my young son, when confronted about going somewhere against his better judgment, to just say, "Because I want to," or, "Because I don't want to." It's inarguable. What can you say to that?

Are you worried that you might sound ignorant when defending your choice? Embarrassment is a prime motivator in ignoring our own opinions sometimes. It's one reason I think people prefer to stay within their own social class. Ever know anyone who was uncomfortable in a setting because it was "too fancy" or "too cheap"? A five-star rating is great for some and not for everybody. Thank goodness we have lots of options.

We are not always uncomfortable with our aesthetic choices. We seem to be able to buy a car without advice from our entire social world. We are even pretty good at resisting commercials (privately). We choose the color, style, and design because the car choice is not considered an art choice. The decision, therefore, falls in the safe zone. Not much risk. It is well presumed that we all have individual tastes and decisions when it comes to buying the ride we like.

The same seems true for clothing choices. In fact, we are encouraged to be true to our individualistic tastes. Some are known for their style, and it becomes a useful signature brand. All well and good. There is, of course, the trend change every year as we receive marketing messages about what is in and what is out. There are folks who care about that, and there are people who just go with what they like.

Your art instinct muscle may not have been exercised regularly in a long time and may be weak at first. In fact, it may be totally resistant. This is a normal reaction. Expect to have to remind yourself of why you are trying new things. We are all a little shaky on new turf with new challenges. One old voice in your head we have not discussed may be Ms. Perfectionism. Her first name is Persistent. Ms. Persistent Perfectionism will ask you over and over to examine your conclusions, your judgments, your efforts. And her cousin Jack Procrastination will slip by her side to tell you that you are just not ready to make these changes.

Yes, you are. You are already making changes if you have read this far. This book made its way to you for a reason. Something inside said there might be a message here for you. I hope that with even one small change, you will feel the first step in the right direction is worth it. There is great satisfaction in getting something you just love. I hope that is happening for you already.

COLOR AND YOUR REACTIONS TO IT

We all have immediate reactions to color. That is another simple human trait. Trying to figure out the art that early man made is filled with speculation. It is fun to figure out what was meant by the cave paintings that have been discovered. Some people think cavemen made the original stop sign. Cavemen filled their mouths with red berry juice. They placed their open hand on the cave wall and blew the juice over it using their hand as a stencil. The effect? A perfect print of their hand with red color all around it. It may have been the first stop sign.

Were they trying to point the way in the cave for fellow travelers? It used to be thought they were just doing that for art's sake. There is no way to prove anything, of course. It's all speculation but fun to think about. Red is an interesting choice, probably dictated by what was around the caveman's environment. Maybe berries were rare, found only seasonally and prized. Or maybe they thought it was a stunning, attention-getting color! It is. The color red means stop in our culture and has other meanings, as do all colors.

WE ALL HAVE FAVORITE COLOR CHOICES

Look at the choices people make in their daily lives regarding color. I think all will agree that color is a major component of art, even in its absence at times (film noir). What draws us to colors? Why, and for what reasons?

What's your favorite color and why?

Do you actually have a favorite? Or do you like them all? Or do you like one today and another one tomorrow, as is sometimes the case?

Make some notes about what strikes you about colors generally:

Specifically:
Red.

Blue.

Yellow.

Green.

White.

Black.

Pastels.

Bold colors.

What color(s) are you wearing right now?

Do you often wear that color or those colors?

Do you notice people treat you differently when wearing a certain color?

Do you drive a "signature color" car?

Use this time to jot down any other thoughts that come up for you about colors.

THE LANGUAGE OF COLOR

The language of color is fun to think about as well. Colors cause immediate reactions. There is a sort of vocabulary to color, though there is no glossary anywhere with rules about what goes best together or how a color functions when next to another color. There are studies that suggest we have psychological (and instinctual) reactions to colors. That's all, thank goodness. Artists then are free to use color any way they choose.

Part of our art awareness journey is to really explore color and its meaning for us as individuals. Colors trigger meaning for us.

Red is visceral, like blood; it also says, WARNING! STOP! Red is always attention-getting and noisy. There was a trend years ago to make restaurants and kitchens bright red as it was thought to enhance appetite. Perhaps one with a hearty appetite might like to eliminate red if that is the case!

Light blue, on the other hand, reminds us of the sky, fair weather, freedom, and joyful, happy, pleasant times.

Dark blue may spell midnight, mysterious, pond-like deep feelings, quiet, deep, and dark water, like the ocean.

And how do you feel about yellow? Caution? Is there a reason stop signs are not yellow? Yellow is the sunny color, of course, indicating happiness. Think of the happy-face emoji that is so common. How would that have looked if it were green (bilious)? Purple (sick)? Pink (blushing)? You get the point.

Green means GO! It signifies health, foliage, calm, serenity, and peace to most cultures. It is placid and pleasant. Calming and soothing. There are shades, tones, and pastel versions of colors too, with entirely different effects upon us. Sage is a very different green than emerald, for instance.

I have always felt a little sorry for so many American workers in colorless corporate environments with nothing but beige and gray cubicles. A little color could make for a happier workforce. It can produce desired, satisfying feelings that I would think all employers would desire.

START PAYING ATTENTION TO COLORS

See what moods certain colors put you in. Pay attention to when you are annoyed at a color that doesn't match your mood. FEELING color is a great, new way to go through life.

Assign yourself a day to just experience color. Start with your morning routine, what clothes you choose, and for what reasons. Give yourself time for notes as you go through your normal day. Just look for color and look at color. Register your reactions. You will be surprised at how colors affect or reflect your mood.

Helpful hint: If you squint your eyes, the scene you are looking at will blur, and the details will be lost. Artists use this all the time to check composition, for instance, when the detail distracts from basic forms and colors. Use squinting on your color exploration day and discover what you are actually reacting to. Losing the details simplifies things, and the color should be more striking in its impact on you.

Jot down any thoughts you may have about this.

SOME STUDIES OF COLOR

Science research has shown that the color of the walls in mental institutions matters. Those already depressed can't stand a sudden change to cheerful yellow walls. The gap is too big—the jump too large and difficult for someone in the dumps. Practitioners found that they could gradually lighten and brighten the walls in slight and subtle increments and raise the mood of the patients with more joyful colors—as long as it was done in increments and not all at once.

Another example is what has been referred to as "drunk-tank pink." There is a shade of pink magenta that weakens people. Jailers discovered that those thrown into the drunk tank were less aggressive when the walls were painted this shade of pink.

I have often wondered about athletes who choose a line of athletic shoes that are of that same pink color. When they then lose the match or the race, I wonder; if it is scientifically true there is a cause-and-effect relationship with this color on strength, then why not choose a strength-enhancing color to wear? I sure would.

And what would that color be? What "strong" colors come to mind?

Think of those strong colors. Do you feel differently when you choose one color over another? Do you consider that sometimes that is not the right color for this day or this mood?

Jot down any thoughts that strike you about how color affects you.

Start paying more attention to color and what you like.

ARE COLORS GOOD OR BAD?

"Going green" has psychological overtones, as does "feeling blue" or "red hot!" Pay attention to references to color and what they do to you. By being selective about the colors that touch you, you can enrich life. Good and bad feelings may only be that. Some colors remind us of good and bad memories. Clothiers certainly know this, as do makeup artists, fashion designers, seasonal trend predictors, etc.

During some seasons, colors are presented in clothing that will never suit me. I could probably wear them, but I don't like them. I don't like the way they make me feel when I look in the mirror. However, it is nice that there is something for everyone; people get their own season. Start looking at colors differently because they really do matter in your life.

Be sure to have fun the whole way. This should not feel like a chore. If it does, it may not be right for you. A self-development journey like this one may be a lifelong project that you are only beginning, so don't overthink it. Try not to be too hard on yourself. Growth takes time; you've lived a lifetime up until now with other beliefs. Give this a chance but in a gentle, kind way to yourself. This is not a mandatory course you have to pass to have a happy life. It's an opportunity.

CHAPTER 16

ART AWAKENING

SO, HOW DO YOU GET THESE INSTINCTS YOU WERE BORN with to become your active radar when you start looking at art again? You pay attention. You begin by looking for ways to think art might belong in your life. If you feel there is no room for art, then the journey is stymied from the start. How much room are we talking about? Not a lot. Especially at first. Like getting ready for any growth, we have to do some clearing of the mind.

Clearing the mind is opening up to new possibilities. You got this book because something inside you (your *instincts*) said to you there might be something here for you. Now, you can create a space for the growth that can come about as we travel the road to sharpened intuition. Getting rid of old beliefs clears the mind and makes space for new thoughts. Clearing physical space can do the same for new items that might occupy art space in your home.

A CREATIVE ENVIRONMENT
MAKES LIFE MORE SATISFYING!

We need a creative environment to keep our art instincts alive, whether mental or physical. It should be protected and fostered in every way, certainly for children, but for adults too. It allows for more problem-solving, which is a main component of creativity. Looking at a problem, thinking of ideas, and solving the problem is a creative endeavor, no matter the subject.

An objective for us here, as you will find out, is to help you, dear reader, provide an enriching set of life experiences for yourself to help you grow in art appreciation. By enlivening your original art instincts and surrounding yourself with stuff you just love, you will feel comforted and more joyful each day. We are affected by what we see daily, and if we don't like it, we tend to stop looking. We become numb to our surroundings. Instead, let's provide a rich tapestry of small pleasures that you can treasure every day. I was very lucky to learn early on that small joys make big joys. How can we set up a more creative mental environment to help us get more art back into our lives? Think of any mental changes that you may need. What's holding you back?

What can you do to change your mind? Talk to someone? Or *don't* talk to anyone about this?

Meditate on what life would be like if you considered art essential, and jot down your thoughts here:

We pay attention to what we think is essential. Can you get creative about art ideas?

What problems must you solve to create more mental space for art?

We need a creative environment, not only in our minds but in our physical surroundings.

GO THROUGH YOUR HOUSE RIGHT NOW!
If not physically, do this exercise mentally: Go through your house right now and look at the decorations you have at present, one by one. For each item, ask yourself the all-important question: do I like it? If not, why are you keeping it? Some answers might be, someone special gave it to me, it cost a *lot*, and I don't want to waste that money, or I don't know what else to do with it. Are you being held captive by these old notions? Does it really matter how much it once cost if you hate it? Does it help anyone for you to keep it?

There are lots of places to donate art. If it cost a lot, give it to a hospital or nursing home and take the value of it off your taxes. Charitable giving is a great way to get things into circulation where they will be appreciated.
List some items you dislike.

Is it really fair for you to keep those items? Give them to someone who really would appreciate them; they deserve a good home!

Do you know someone who has always wanted one of those items? Can you part with it?

Don't you deserve to have only things you love around you? Or are you relegated to other's hand-me-downs? Freeing yourself of these unwanted items makes room in your environment for your own expression.

CAUTION: THE SHOULDS ARE OFTEN NEARBY!

Be aware of all the "shoulds" that may still remain in your brain from your old ways of thinking, and be careful of developing new "shoulds."

This book is to help you have only one rule: *do I like it?* We are not trying to set up a new set of rules. We do that sometimes (certainly with dieting), where we box ourselves in with our new thinking just the way we had done before. Now we have a new set of rules. Oops! The objective of this book is freedom of choice, no restrictions.

How is your self-doubt doing now?

Have you learned anything? If so, what?

Did you have different opinions about each of those objects? Good? Bad? Keep it? Throw it?

GIVE YOURSELF PERMISSION TO MAKE WRONG CHOICES

After all, what is the actual risk? Some hurt feelings, resentment, or regretting the choice afterward? Cut yourself some slack. Your art instinct muscle hasn't been exercised regularly; it may be weak at first. And there is no time limit; take all the time you need. You may need to go slowly at first.

WARNING: Fast is always better than slow. Your initial reaction when you come upon something is your best gut reaction. Don't give yourself too much time to think about it. Here's why: you won't get back to it, or you will talk yourself out of the initial evaluation. You may remind yourself of the old rationales, the fears of what may happen if you make your favorite choice. It will start to feel riskier than it really is. Remember, we are still approval-seeking beings. Mostly, I find that people don't care if you pass things along. You can downsize or outgrow things and phases in your life, change color schemes, and put it all in storage in case the person who got you this piece comes to visit. Most understand these changes.

You are not the same person you used to be. Deciding what you do and don't like is defining; you are not the same person who bought that thing years ago. Allow yourself to be the You that you are right now and get rid of Old You! Furthermore, no one has to even know you are going through this pro-cess; relieve yourself of the pressure of what others are going to think about this. Life is not a dress rehearsal. If you want to share publicly what you are doing and how it feels, that's fine, of course. I will bet you will get positive reactions. Most people will think, "Yeah, I need to go through my house too." Everyone complains about having too much stuff and wishes they would do something about it. And the BONUS is: you get to keep what you like. Ah, freedom!

LOOKING VERSUS SEEING

We all think we are seeing, well, all the time. But have you ever had the experience of looking but not perceiving? Did you ever try to compare two photos when challenged to discover what is missing in one of them? *That* is seeing.

We often don't perceive, and this is especially true of things that are habitually in our environment. We stopped seeing what's in that poster in the dining room years ago! Have you ever had someone ask you why you have something, and when they describe it, you realize they are seeing something entire-ly different from what you see? That is seeing: the perception of that object or scene in its entirety. We think we are seeing the whole thing, but it takes awareness to realize we are glanc-ing over the sight of something. This is apparent when people learn to draw. They often draw what they think the object looks like. Learning to draw means learning how to really see.

I'll say again, reawakening our senses makes life richer. It is "living in the NOW," urging us to be present . . . Don't just attend; *be there*. It's that wonderful feeling on the beach when you suddenly notice the wind is blowing your hair, and you don't care; in fact, you love it.

Can you think of other examples of feelings like this?

I'm not talking about physically seeing, as in your eyes do their job. Good eyesight is a wonderful advantage, of course. I am talking about seeing what is really there, not what you think you see. This often shows up when people start to draw. They draw what they think they see instead of what they really see. It is just a matter of recognizing that perceptions are altered by our thoughts. In the next chapter, we will examine what it means to learn to draw.

CHAPTER 17

WE DRAW CONCLUSIONS!

WE ARE QUICK TO COME TO CONCLUSIONS WITHOUT A LOT OF facts and evidence. As I have underscored, we are particularly vulnerable when we respect another's opinion. As we become even harsher critics of ourselves, we join with the Art Assassin to prove once and for all that art is not for us. Here's what I have learned about when children decide they are not talented: it usually has to do with drawing.

THE REASON CHILDREN CONCLUDE
THEY CAN'T "DO" ART

In Chapter 3, we saw that children usually decide whether or not they can draw around the third grade. Before this revelation, children's drawings are magical—to them and to us. That early way of seeing and expressing is just wonderful. I was once shown a drawing by a five-year-old that was a horizontal blank sheet of paper with just four vertical lines from top to bottom drawn in—nothing else! He told the teacher as she asked him about it, "I didn't have room for the rest of the elephant." Now, that is totally charming. This is a kid who knows how to think big! And it didn't matter that there wasn't room for the whole elephant. Later, for most children, it begins to matter. Fourth graders begin to want their drawings to be real, for everyone to see. When that doesn't happen, they start to give up on being an artist.

Have you ever thought, "I can't draw!"? Many times, if I ask someone if they are artistic, they answer, "I can't draw!" To them, this is the measure of being an artist. Now, we know that there is a lot of visual art that is not based on drawing. I suggest this conclusion by adults comes from those early decisions that there are a few talented people who seem to be able to draw, and therefore, they are destined to become artists, but "not me."

Let's talk about drawing. I have maintained that if you can write at all, you can draw. That is proof that your eyes and hands work. I have good handwriting, not because I am talented at handwriting but because I had a good teacher. Everyone can learn anything if they are taught right. Sometimes, it is the teacher, not the student.

As a young child, I was taught the Palmer method of handwriting. This was an ingenious system to produce good handwriting. Like Mr. Miyagi taught Daniel in *The Karate Kid*, we were taught to make oval lines with our hands, spiraling first in one direction (wax on!) and then the other (wax off!). We did this for weeks with penciled ovals on paper, teaching our little hands motor control to be able to make a series of connected ovals and then to be able to reverse them with the result that they looked identical, like rolls of barbed wire across the page.

By the way, children do love to learn a skill and what is required of them to perfect that skill. I think that is magical. A sense of pride comes with achievement, teaching for achievable results. On the student's level.

After perfecting ovals-on and ovals-off for weeks, we then learned that the letter *a* was simply one oval with a stick by its side. Magic! *b* was just as fun! An oval with a longer, taller stick on the other side. It all made so much sense. *c* was only part of an oval, and *d*, well, there was that longer, taller stick, only this time, it was on the other side! Amazing. See? Not hard. We had the motor control from drawing all those ovals. Now we had the system. We had success. Everyone learned to make some form of ovals and sticks. We saw how it worked. And we could do it.

These days, I am sorry to say that "keyboarding" has taken the place of handwriting. There's not much personality in the QWERTY keyboard, and people berate themselves, saying their handwriting is terrible as a result. More apologies for what is not their fault.

Much like how phonics is essential to learning to read, hand and eye control are essential to good handwriting. My suggestion here is that I could teach you to draw if I gave you a system that always works. This takes it out of the realm of only the talented can draw.

Let's draw a face. Right now. You know the head is just like the shape of an egg. There is a rounded, fuller end to the egg and a pointy end.

1. Draw an egg-shaped oval on your paper with the pointy end down. That is the shape of a head. Remember, an egg is not an oval but a pointy oval, round on the top and pointy on the bottom.

2. Now draw a line horizontally across the egg from left to right, halfway down. This is the first line.

3. Now draw a line across the egg from left to right, halfway down between the first line and the pointed bottom tip of the egg. The second line!

4. Now draw a horizontal line across the egg from the left to the right, halfway down from the second line. Line #3.

5. Now draw a fourth horizontal line halfway down again, across, from left to right.

6. One more time, draw a fifth horizontal line halfway down if you wish. This line is indicated by a dotted line in the illustration coming up! And shows the finishing touch!

7. Voilà! The structure is set! Watch this.

A person's eyes go on the first top horizontal line you drew halfway down. Line #1.

Eyes are not two marbles but two almonds, one on each side on the horizontal line.

The second line down is the bottom tip of the nose; draw a shallow U shape. This is the horizontal shadow under the tip of the nose. A shallow and not very wide bottom tip of the nose will do. You can embellish, personalize, or individualize later.

The third line is for the mouth. Flatten a letter M shape so that it is very shallow. That is the upper lip, sitting on that line.

The fourth line is the top of the chin shape, halfway between the upper lip M-shaped line and the bottom of the egg.

A fifth line can be inserted between the third and fourth (see illustration) the dotted line indicates the bottom boundary of the bottom lip. Another shallow U shape will indicate that. Lips are all different; use your instincts! You will know how to add this feature. It is different for every person.

Can you see it?

Wait! What about the ears and hair, and neck?

The ears go between the first and second lines. This is the placement of most ears on the head. This varies quite a lot among individuals. Now that you know where they are *supposed* to be, everything becomes a variation on the theme. You already know the shape of ideal ears. The fun part is that everyone's ears are so different! Flat or sticking out, you decide. Draw it to suit the subject.

Fill in the shallow M upper lip shape because upper lips are in darker shadow under the nose, that shadow defines the lips. That makes the face more realistic. The bottom lip is in light, and less delineated.

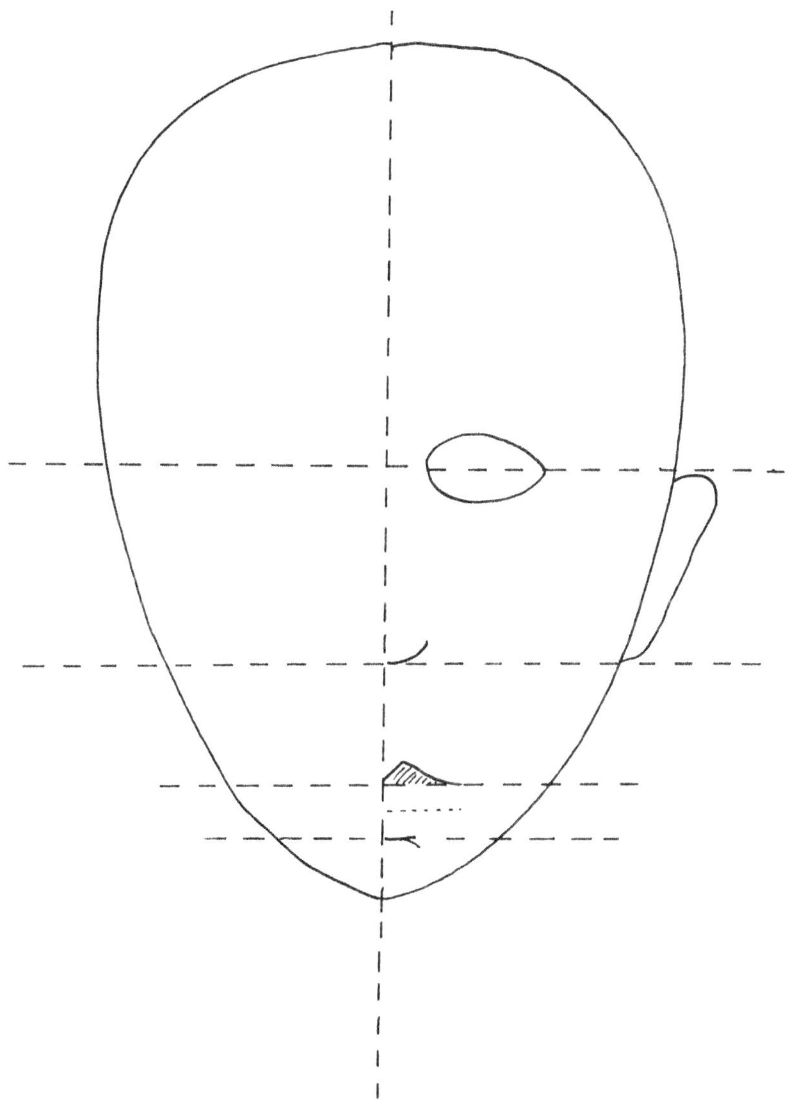

Make a pedestal for the head by adding two vertical lines for the neck. (On either side of the chin, of course.) The neck is like a collar; a little curve in the side lines makes it seem more real and human. Round the line under the chin . . . like a column supporting the face.

When you are ready to cover this head with hair, which is the next fun part, you will see what is wrong with most face drawings. Hair does not sit on top of the egg!

It covers a lot of the top half of the rounded section of the egg—most of the top half of the egg is forehead and hair! So have fun with it! You really can go wild with this feature, as you will note as you observe the population's choices of hairdos.

You can add some eyebrows now. In fact, you can embellish this basic drawing any way you please. Draw it over and over and play with the idea that you now know the basic proportions of any human head. All the rest now is just accommodating personal differences and preferences.

You can see how portraiture works, how a portrait artist is someone capable of seeing individual differences and drawing them. The caricaturist has an extremely acute way of seeing and exaggerating differences. You have just learned the basics, however, from which that artist begins.

Congratulations! *YOU CAN DRAW!*

You've done it! Everything is so much simpler if you have a system. Now you can always draw a face! It all begins with these basic shapes with necessary changes to reflect characteristics. More or less hair. Longer nose. Eyes further apart or narrowly seated.

I have done this exercise with children using hard-boiled eggs on which we drew the lines and added some red-marker lips and modeling clay for ears and hair . . . So fun! One reason I knew you could do this is because I saw third graders do it. Remember our decisions about drawing in the third grade or so? Well, now you have picked up where you left off!

If you had been taught some simple drawing lessons, then you might have done better as a child. Some kids figure some of it out by themselves. The art educational system often seems to be to 1) set up a project and 2) let them go for it. There could be a lot more. Good teaching, in my view, lets everyone succeed. It's not always the kid's fault.

> *"If a child can't learn the way we teach,*
> *maybe we should teach the way they learn."*
> *—Ignacio Estrada*

Do you think drawing is a bit more fun now? Reflect on your experience of learning to draw a face.

CHAPTER 18

ART TAKES MANY FORMS

LET ME ASK YOU A QUESTION. IS DOODLING ART? MOST OF US doodle. Do you doodle? One of the greatest things about doodling is that we don't call it art, generally. (As a result, we don't have to defend it as art!) Doodling can create a healthy release of emotion and combat boredom, anxiety, frustration, and all the other stressors of life. It has healthful benefits, of course, and it is just plain fun. Does it sound like your inner child might like it? It calms our nerves for lines to wander on a page with no destination. Sometimes whimsical, sometimes fierce, and always expressive. I love it because it lets the imagination go wild. We use it sometimes as a distraction. There is no penalty in a meeting if someone uses their notepad for doodling instead of notes.

Just doodle for a minute. Start with a single line and see where it goes. Just a quick scribble. Scribbling has its own rewards. Remember, you know how to do this! Put something down on the paper; now add to it, and add to that. Remember? Fun, right? Spend as little or as long as you want to do this. Sometimes, a quick little scribble becomes the most profoundly interesting thing! Make several! Today and most days. There is great stress reduction in just doodling. I recommend it.

FOLK ART IS MADE BY FOLKS

There is another fun activity people engage in, which we call folk art. We do call people "folks," right? These are art makers who are not trained artists (it's not a necessary requirement!). Usually, folk art refers to practical items we use in life, dressed up decoratively at the owner's whim. It is referred to as "naive art" by some art historians. However, *naive* might also mean childlike, which fits right in with our definition of the perfect art appreciator. We are growing more and more fond of child-like descriptions. There are lots of examples of exquisite folk art. Quiltmakers come to mind. Native Americans and the Amish come to mind. The thing I am fondest of when it comes to quilts is that the simplest and most uncomplicated ones are often the most fetching. They often tell a story. I am reminded of the map done in quilt technique that showed the way for the Underground Railroad travelers so they could get there and remain safe.

Does this remind you of anyone you know who putters around with some material and comes out with the most amazing results?

Have you ever done anything like this before?

Are there any projects coming to mind that you could work on?

What would it take? Supplies? Time? Money? Encouragement? Permission (from whom and when?)?

MAILBOXES ARE FOLK ART

I once wrote a paper on what people in Michigan were doing with their mailboxes. It seemed to me a prime example of folk art. Changing an otherwise simply useful object into art made it an interesting example that met the definition of folk art. For years, I have known that those in frozen Michigan with long winters usually have hobbies or interests to keep them busy inside for those long, cold months. Many people have basement projects, workshop ideas, or a boat being built in the garage (lots of lakes in Michigan). I always regarded the Michiganders as very creative. Not only could they "make do," fixing things with limited resources sometimes, but they also knew how to have fun with it. It was *so* apparent as I drove the country roads. One example sticks out in my mind as there were two mailboxes at the driveway. One was the regular one, at standard height, and another was on a post about ten feet tall. That was the mailbox for air mail.

Some people painted them interestingly. With all those lakes, fishing is a prominent pastime. There were many fish mailboxes! Now, a fish is an interesting shape, right? Not hard to make at all. They are also about mailbox-shaped! It is so easy to make that all children can do it.

Here's a simple exercise for the children in your life. Have them color basic fish shapes on paper, with as many variations as they can think of, using crayons. Then, mix some blue and white poster paint, thinned with enough water to make a very fluid, thin paint. The children can then use this "pond water" (the thin blue paint) to paint over the fish. Because paint won't stick to crayon wax, the fish emerge from the pond for an effect that delights us all! The technique is called "crayon resist" and is very fun. Let it dry and put it on the fridge!

OTHER FORMS OF ART

There are so many art forms that people are reluctant to call art. For example, lots of parents would like to think video games are *not* art! No matter what you think about the content of video games, they are definitely a form of visual art. And in many cases, a brilliant form of visual art. They connect with players on a visceral level. They communicate! The excitement and challenge of winning the game enhances the experience, of course. Even without the game element, the drawings, colors, and action animation are fascinating. One can hardly NOT look at it. It is magnetic and very compelling. Add to that the fun it provides, and voilà—an emotional experience that is very magnetic.

What about cartoons? Are they art? You bet they are! Today's generation takes for granted that any image can be generated at any time on a computer. Think of early Disney animations, where artists followed chipmunks, sketching every signature move chipmunks make every day. The result? Chip and Dale. Who knew a rabbit with classy moves could be as fetching as Bugs Bunny? Every human emotion has been expressed in cartooning over the years. Didn't we say that art is communication through emotions?

We relate to these characters who only exist to entertain us. And entertain, they do! Some of the most fun times in life can come from a mere line image astutely pointing to one of our human flaws or triumphs. Art can be truth-revealing as it expresses human nature.

You may also notice that storytelling using pictures is always better than just words. "A picture is worth a thousand words" is not an idle saying. Remember, we said that thoughts come to our brains as pictures first! Then words! Therefore, our first impression of a topic is pictorial. When we are helped along by the graphic artist (think trademarks, ads, logos, commercials, billboards, truck signs, etc.), we get an immediate boost in the effectiveness of the message.

Thought teaser: How long has it been since you read what used to be called the funnies?

YOUR VISUAL LIBRARY

Comic books, graphic novels—*all* cartoons are illustrations that contribute to our visual library. We archive what touches us visually, for use later. One of the goals of this book is to increase your exposure to art and the fun that it brings to you. Think of how fun it must be to be a cartoonist. Here's something you can do today: seek out a cartoon or video game and just look at it. That's all, just look at it.

If it's Saturday, there is a well-known kids' morning activity you might join. Saturday cartoons! See what today's youth are watching, and have some fun yourself. It's another art exposure for you this week.

What did you experience?

Did your inner kid love it?

Did your adult self have an opinion? (Remember, this is not about content; try to leave that out of the equation.)

What drew you in? The color? The drawing techniques?

Did you find it imaginative? Fun? Funny? Clever?

FINE ARTS: WHAT ARE THEY?

Part of the art snob vocabulary is the category of fine arts. Exclusivity is not always just in the art patron but also in the artist which definitely propagates the Art Myth. Every artist loves to be known as "a fine artist." The category generally holds paintings, drawings, sculpture, and architecture. Some cultures would include poetry. Eastern cultures say that painters must also be poets to truly be artists, which is interesting when you consider our haiku example from Chapter 3. Both mediums require the same sensitivity.

There is always a discussion among fine artists asserting that crafts are not art, and sometimes other things like manuscripts or textiles are excluded as well. Does it matter? Who cares?

Are crafts really art? Our definition of art implies that if you react well to it, if it speaks to you, then yes, your art instincts would define it as art. And if you are being true to your art instincts, you shouldn't care how it is labeled, right?

This new recognition of art as emotional communication is only meant to free you from all art labels. If one opens up the art category and removes all the labels, there is a lot more fun out there and many more options for the artistic experience. That is one of your new objectives. Seek out art wherever you can find it. It only matters to the elitist whether or not it is called art. If you like it, include it in your life.

THE SECRET SOCIETY OF ART MAKERS

Did you know there is such a society as Art Makers Anonymous? (Ha-ha, AMA for short). People all over the nation are making art without telling anyone, not even themselves, that is what they are doing. It is a *huge, behind-the-scenes secret society*. It's very prevalent. It exists all over the world. You know some of its members, and maybe you are one.

It is not acknowledged formally, because then the makers would have to label their efforts as being art. We desperately want art in our lives because art really does make us happy. The issue always becomes, as the myth dictates, that if it is called "real art," it has to follow the elitist rules to be valid. But that is not so. People know it in their hearts, so they make non-art objects. Regularly.

CHAPTER 19

LABELING ART

MANY PEOPLE ARE TOTALLY INTIMIDATED BY EVEN THE WORD "art," let alone the word "artist." They do not consider what they do as art or artistry. They don't want to think that they might, even for a minute, BE an artist. By naming the result as "art," one claims it as art, and then it must be defended. It makes people very uncomfortable if what they are making is put into that rarefied-air category that has such a cloud of mystery around it. The maker might also have to have the pedigree to gain respect for the object and for the maker. It's easier to just avoid it. By avoiding the label of art, one can get away with anything.

It is rumored that Alexander Calder would not refer to his creations, now famously known as mobiles, as "art." He said he was simply making objects. Not art objects. Just objects. That was very clever since he never had to defend this new style of art object as being real art. Today, his creations are among the greatest art objects in the world. Hah. Interesting that he just created them from imagination because he liked them. Did he follow his instincts?

We are going to talk about how people feel that they need to justify themselves when they label art objects. It can be very intimidating, and often causes consternation just because of the art label.

WE MAKE JUDGMENTS ABOUT ART ALL THE TIME

Listen to the ways in which people talk about the artistic endeavors they engage in without calling it art:

"Yeah, I'm good at gardening, but it's not art . . . Well, Japanese gardens are more like art, but not mine." (Oh really? You created the visual sensation by deciding what and where to plant, right? It is in the order you created, right? It's lovely to look at, right? Doesn't that make it art?)

"My daughter likes to feel like a princess, so I usually add a little extra to her dresses when I sew them so she will feel special. She likes twirling about."

"I just couldn't find a blueprint for the room I wanted over the garage, so I just did it."

"My car is my pride and joy; I wanted to personalize it so people around town would say, 'I know that white car with the braces drawn on it! That's the dentist's car!'"

"There's something about your own mark on a musical instrument to make it stand out. I love the loud colors I put on my guitar. It goes with loud music!"

"Sometimes I wonder why a person would put drapes like that in a room like this. Can't they see that the colors don't work well? I would have chosen blue."

Do you recognize innovation, imagination, problem-solving, and the freedom to make aesthetic choices? These are the ingredients of art making. These examples do not fit into the Art Myth and are the exception. There is a lot of art enthusiasm shown by the hobbyists' efforts. These are people using their art instincts and making art without worry.

So, when do we call it art?

Can you think of any other forms of art that people do that are sometimes not considered "real art"?

ZENTANGLE

If you have never heard of or tried Zentangle, you might like to try and discover this as well. It's a brilliant method that is taught all over the United States as of this writing in 2023. Zentangle can bring very rewarding results and is easy to do. There is a certification available to teach the method for students to get the most out of it. However, the original book describing the idea is a great way for anyone to start. See the Additional Related Reading section at the back of this book.

What is Zentangle? Well, it is tangling lines together to discover shapes and make a work of art out of it. See the additional reading list to discover what it is and how to do it. Remember we talked about doodling? Doodling is great! It can unlock all sorts of feelings. When combined with color and definition or just left in black and white, the end result can be very appealing. It has a way of looking very skilled, and it's a great confidence booster if you like the idea of learning more about drawing. I highly recommend it.

Untangling a scribble is problem-solving. Remember, problem-solving—coming up with innovations when presented with a challenge—takes imagination and builds the creative muscle.

I very much applaud the invention of Zentangle and its founders for their recognition that making art this way is very rewarding. Try it yourself sometime.

Let's pursue the idea that art can be found in unexpected places. Think of activities that you might enjoy or have around you that are potentially art-full.

What other art awareness exercises can you think of to add to your life?

TRY FRAMING YOUR VIEW OF THE WORLD

Photographers frame their view of the world all the time, of course. They see the world framed like a photograph. You most probably have, too, since the invention of the smartphone camera. We look and experience our world differently now because of this new technology. It's a good thing. We look through a camera lens, which squares off the view and frames it for us. In fact, we sometimes don't actually participate in the event except as spectators through our cameras. Documenting and recording the event takes priority over enjoying it. We take a step back to see the whole picture and make sure all the important elements are in the picture. It makes for some great family memories. It is easy to do.

The technique of framing has been used by artists for centuries. If you make an L shape with your fingers, you have half a frame without the camera. Using just your fingers, the second hand completes the frame, and you can focus on a subject more clearly. This is useful when you want to pull out of a scene only what is important to you. If you draw or paint that scene, it is essential that the important elements look pleasing to the eye. This technique allows the artist to judge whether or not it would make a good subject.

How is this relevant to you today? It is an easy way to see things differently. You can do it anywhere, with just your hands framing the scene to distill everything into an artistic view. Why? Because it sharpens your seeing skills. You start to see shapes and colors and not just the obvious subject matter. Suddenly, it is not just a girl with a hat, but the hat is more important than the girl. Now it may look different because you have shifted the focus.

Can you use your smartphone to help you do this? Of course. It is actually easier. I only suggest your hands because you always have them ready, whereas the camera may be in the car! Or your purse. Or your pocket. Just lift your hand and use that L shape to cut away the things that don't matter and see if it looks like art.

I'll bet you have framed many a sunset! See? You are already good at it.

SQUINTING IS NOT JUST FOR WHEN THE SUN IS IN YOUR EYES

I mentioned squinting as a technique once before when discussing color. Squinting can change the way you perceive shapes and colors. If you want to eliminate the details of a complex scene, all you have to do is squint. Something magical happens when squinting at a scene. The first observable effect, of course, is that the scene is blurred. This automatically takes out all the fine lines and complexities that muddy up the view. By blurring in this way, you only see the most obvious: the shapes and colors.

Why does this matter? Because you can then perceive the most dominant features. This is helpful when placing an object in a room. If you are not sure where on the wall to place the picture, try squinting. Just look at the negative space and see if it balances with the positive space. If it is too far left or too high or low, you will see it better if you get rid of the details. We are so easily distracted that we focus on the wrong things sometimes. You will be more aware of the feel of the room or the impact of the color of the drapes if you squint and just look at the main objects.

Try it. If something seems too hard or too complex, try squinting and taking out the subtleties and simplifying the scene. You will then know, by your intuitions, what looks good. It's a fun and easy technique. Try squinting at the front door of your home. Do the bushes dominate the front entrance? Does the color of the door really work there? Does it seem that all you can see is your car in front of the entrance? What could make it look better? A wreath? A pot of flowers? A big rock? Trim away some of that foliage? What could you add? What could you subtract?

This also works for your own clothing. Does that color make you look top-heavy? Your shoulders too broad? Your ankles too narrow? Fashionistas know these things.

Balance is one of the fundamentals of art that we react to without really thinking about it. It is instinctive to have things in balance. Try squinting to see how something really looks.

Think of some more exercises you can do in daily life to notice art. Where and when could you do this?

The office?

School?

Work?

Home?

At the mall?

On a walk?

In the car?

On the weekend?

With a friend?

Come up with more ideas.

CHAPTER 20

Your Art Journey

Stay on your art journey. Seeing and not just looking, enjoying instead of just living with stuff, and exploring art instead of just meaning to should be adding more fun to your life. If you have had a little bit of success in recognizing that art might be missing in your life, and it's been gone too long, you can easily keep going. Commit to listening to your instincts.

Your journey should feel free and easy. No assignments. A commitment to keep learning with no commitment to a structure, a schedule, or anything that risks setting you up for disappointment when not followed through.

The inspired moments, when you remember that they're potential learning moments, are what you are looking to keep in your life going forward. It's a process that takes time. Loose, unorganized time. Now, the caveat must be that if you are an organized person who needs structure and scheduling, then by all means, schedule in some museum or gallery time, trips with the kids, or friends for lunches that include art. It's your journey. In your own time. In your own way.

Find out what you like to do now, as you are now, at this age. We have revisited what you may have liked in the past or left behind. There is a lot of life ahead of you. You don't even have to do much more of this. We are learning to trust our feelings. The funny thing is that sometimes when we let go of something, it comes back. It sometimes comes back at a more fortuitous time. So perhaps the best thing is to just remember you can always be on this journey whenever you want. You'll know when. You will know what to do then, instinctively.

Just see things through your new eyes with your old instincts. Maybe it will just be in front of the greeting cards at the supermarket. Or in the garden where things go stitching, stitching.

IT'S OKAY TO CHALLENGE YOURSELF

You can challenge yourself now to go to places that were formerly forbidden because of old beliefs. What about an expensive art gallery? Go in your old clothes! See if you know what you like (and if you do, then it doesn't matter how much it costs). Could you just go in to see what's in there? It might be interesting.

It's fun to see what's new and what's being advertised at what prices. It's fun to see that there may be better stuff at the flea market for a bargain than this gallery's art. It's also fun to see why they are so expensive. The artwork of hard-to-acquire artists can be fascinating. What a good exercise for the art-minded! (That's you now!)

Go into an art gallery or a museum and ask yourself: What is it that makes this art so appealing? The size? The color? The story? The lack of story? The atmosphere? The mood? The combination of shapes? The fact that it's off balance? What is it?

It—that mysterious quality we speak of with awe. She has *it* (star quality); he's got *it* (charm, magnetism, charisma)! Well, artwork has *it* too. The only thing is that *it* is not general, but specific to us. We get *it* from the work. Did the artist put *it* in there for us? Maybe, maybe not. The fact is, we know *it* when we see *it*.

FIND MORE WAYS TO LOOK AND TO SEE

Go where the action is. Listen to an artist speak (online videos, virtual talks, TV specials, interviews, etc.). There is a lot out there if you go looking for it. Encourage yourself to keep finding new ways to explore art. Bookstores, clubs, movie theaters, stage. Remember in the beginning, I spoke of the practice of reawakening your art instincts? Well, this is the practice. Putting yourself in front of art. I mentioned greeting cards, but what about wrapping paper, paint stores, tile shops, and carpets from all over the world? Great art stuff! Daily little art stuff, replacement art stuff, furniture, patio and garden art, delicate stuff, and strong stuff. A garden gate! Hanging stuff, standing stuff, bold and subtle stuff.

Finding and seeing art stuff will make you stronger. You will have a greater reference library of what turns you on. As you begin to collect images you like in your brain, with a peg to put it on, as Piaget suggests, you build a reservoir of enjoyment to draw upon. All of this informs your art instincts about what you really like. Give it the chance to enlarge and enrich you. You will love the good feelings it can produce.

By the way, the great educator and thinker Piaget suggested we only retain those thoughts that can connect to previous information collected in our brain. Having a peg to put another idea on is essential for real learning. In this book, we have given you some foundational pegs on which to put your future art exposure learning experiences. You should retain the new art knowledge you have acquired as you build toward a greater appreciation of art.

ONE EXPERIENCE BUILDS ON ANOTHER

Call to action: support your Art Angel; keep going. Time for the Art Assassin to get "outta here." You really have to keep giving your Art Angel some good feedback. She's fairly strong, considering you gave her little acknowledgment or positive action results for her faith in you for some time. You were actually busy feeding the Art Assassin.

Like all voids that get filled, you will find that the less you listen to the Art Assassin, and the more attention you give Art Angel, the less you hear from Assassin's wickedness. Time for her to get quiet and take a nap. You know she's wrong. She's just a made-up voice from all those wrong comments you heard as a child. Those beliefs went up in smoke as you stoked the fire, pursuing your instincts and letting your Art Self warm up! You're not in danger anymore.

It can be a slippery slope if you ever let in Self-Doubt, the Art Assassin's kid brother. We used to say, "One ounce of doubt, you're out!" Doubt and confidence have a hard time residing together. Choose. You know which one serves you better.

Mostly, have fun! As you begin to form likes and dislikes, you may feel the need to share with a buddy. Take a friend to look at your new discovery. Now, in the past, this was shaky ground where what the friend might say would affect you. By now, you should be feeling more confident in the fact that the friend's opinion is no better than yours.

ARE YOU FEELING IT?

Are your art instincts feeling like good companions now? I hope you now see that you have had unwarranted old beliefs, lots of bad self-talk, and a lack of confidence in choosing art before now. I also hope that you have realized some new beliefs, you've experienced some joy in exploring art around you, and you want to continue. Trusting your instincts should be feeling more comfortable by now. I will be interested to hear how you are doing.

Write some final notes to remind yourself of how far you have come.

MAYBE IT'S TIME FOR THE BIG ONE! GO TO THE MUSEUM!

Museum visits can feel intimidating unless you just refuse to be intimidated. Let your stubborn side reaffirm, "I am just going to go and see what it is all about." With that attitude, you can remain open to what you see. The old way of thinking might have residual thoughts of, "This is the place that holds art, and I don't know anything about art." What a good place to see how well your instincts really work. This is the Olympics of trying out your art instincts.

What are your present feelings about museums?

Do you know of one you could visit? Where and when? Jot down the locations and hours, etc.

Would you prefer to go alone or with a buddy? If with a buddy, who?

Does it cost much?

Plan to make this trip a simple, casual affair. There are no rules to visiting a museum except not touching the artwork.

Let's talk for a minute about why museums exist in the first place. They are reservoirs of what has been done in the past. We know history is important to civilization; this is not an argument regarding history. It is to say, however, that just because it was done in the past, kept, recorded, studied, and documented does not mean it's good.

What? Does that surprise you?

We understand that historians and curators will choose the best of what they find as an example of what was done before our time. Of course, we want to see Greek sculpture. After enough time has passed, we only have a few examples of some eras. Humanity would probably want to keep all examples of an ancient civilization. That seems reasonable.

What about current artworks? First, we most likely do not have the perspective to know what will stand the test of time. There may be a few reasons to put a work of art in a museum. If there is an all-white painting in the art museum or one that is all-black, it is there because it was the natural progression of an idea. Painting hit its zenith in the seventeenth century. After the Renaissance discoveries of extraordinary painting, there was little to do beyond that. Artists became interested in new ways to create meaningful images. Of course, that had to be an all-white and an all-black painting; it was the logical conclusion of painting imagery. It is the museum's job to document all the developments in art because they existed, nothing more. It is a chronology of the evolution of man's art expression.

With that brief background of why museums exist, I encourage you to go to one. The same is true for all museums, by the way, not just art museums. If it is a museum of farm equipment, the fact remains that it is a compilation of the history of farm equipment and the best examples of those machines. You owe it to your art instincts to at least go to one museum.

Some museums will let you take pictures of what you see. In some cases, photo flashes are reputed to hurt paintings. There is generally enough light for a smartphone photo. If you can, take some pictures to keep in your mind's art library of what you have seen. One of our objectives here is to broaden your exposure to all kinds of art. You may want to think about that image later. It's good to have a reference.

THE MUSEUM EXPERIENCE: DID YOU ENJOY IT?
It's useful to make notes about where you went and what it meant to you.
Was it fun?

Did you learn anything new?

What surprised you the most?

What did you like the most?

Did you find anything appalling?

Are you glad you went?

You should feel proud for having given yourself this experience! High five!

CHAPTER 21

REMEMBER TO STAY AWARE

You should be feeling more art aware now. Even if you haven't taken any of these suggestions seriously yet, you should be at least more aware of potential changes in seeing art in a different way.

Take a moment to reflect on what you have learned.

Remember, we are trying to get in touch with emotional responses; how does all of this feel? Is it fun? Scary? Uncomfortable? Relieving? Freeing?

Do you feel more confident in your choices?

What's next? More art noticing is the answer. It is important to keep working on art awareness around you. This can easily become a very natural part of your wandering through the world now. If you have been trying to live consciously aware of what you see, you may also be enjoying the fruits of that labor.

The visual world is an amazing place with delicious treats for your eyes. Take it in as much as you can. Notice the dreary times, too, and feel it all. It will help you translate art. You are broadening your shoulders to hold all of the art impressions you can take. Just remember what you have learned on this journey to reawaken your art instincts.

Be warned that awareness can slip away into old habitual thinking so slyly that we don't even notice it. This is why diet clubs work if members attend weekly sessions to stay motivated. We need reminders of even the concepts we totally understand and take on. That is why most churches would have weekly services. Make these new thought exercises part of your daily rituals so the old beliefs stay away from your door.

REMEMBER, ART'S ALWAYS WITHIN US

There is evidence now that even Neanderthal people used iron ocher as body paint. Was it to identify themselves as part of the tribe? Or for the sheer fun of it? By the way, identifying as part of a tribe is not so farfetched when you consider the body paint many a sports fan has smeared on his face in order to go to a sporting event to cheer and be part of the fan tribe. Right?

I love the notion that people have always wanted to decorate themselves. Whether to beautify, horrify, or identify, it doesn't matter. Clearly, it is always seen as a valuable addition to society. Ask any cosmetic company.

Remember, creativity is within all of us. Is creativity the same thing as art? I would say creativity produces art and that art is the product, not the process. There are fantastic scholarly literary works about the essence of art. They teach what it is and what makes good and bad art. There are other academic discussions on what makes up creativity. These are sound, well-researched studies and theories about artists and their works.

Creativity, of course, is found in all aspects of life. The nature of creativity is generally accepted to include imagination and innovative ideas to apply to a situation to get resolution. Every type of endeavor can have creativity brought to it. Life is full of opportunities for finding and applying new ideas. It's also fun. It's very productive and the reason humanity evolves.

I would also suggest that we are naturally creative. This is another area in which people are confused. A brilliant scientist will tell you he is only following the facts. Yes. True. And the conclusions come from imaginative and innovative application of creative processes. Sometimes, art and science are not that far apart.

We are going to discuss further what makes creative people. I will simply say here that it does not only have to do with being able to draw and paint. That's a simplified explanation that doesn't wash under scrutiny. Mankind would not have evolved to this high degree without the innate creative urge.

REMEMBER THAT ART IS NOT AN ELITIST SUBJECT

This book is not about being creative. It is about your natural responses to everything you encounter. We trust other instincts, such as warnings about danger. When it comes to art, however, we have learned certain views that make us feel that only a select few really know about art and, therefore, are qualified to judge it. It became an elitist sport in society for a lot of reasons. Later in the book, we will talk more about the Art Myth we have accepted. Our goal here was always to acknowledge some old beliefs we may have acquired about art that don't serve us any longer.

Remember what we said about the power of art? It lifts us up! That is its main purpose. From a musical point of view, it is one thing to play all the notes on the page. It is another to make music! See, the thing is, your inner nature knows the difference. That's the point of reawakening our instincts. We are not talking about technical prowess here. Many people are proficient technicians and are not really making art. True art speaks to our inner nature, our higher selves.

Sometimes, it has been pointed out, art is serendipitous. Artists often call this a "happy accident." That is, they didn't really mean to put it there. The trick for the artist, however, is to recognize when they have hit upon something that resonates in a profound way for the viewer. If it improves the work, leave it there. Recognizing an element as being art calls for the artist to listen to their own inner voice. The happy accident cannot be recognized and used if the artist doesn't see it as a way to bring the viewer the message. That is always the point. Communication. Unique expression that communicates is the objective.

CHAPTER 22

Awaken to Art Opportunities

Your art instincts are coming to life . . . Now what? What do you do with this new awareness? Pass it along. You are able to influence others just as they have influenced you in your life. The difference here, though, is that the intention and the effect will be positive. By balancing the negative effects you have seen in your life and changing your own life, you can now model for others what more art in one's life can mean. It is significant.

Others do want to know about what you are learning, of course. If you are a private person who would never share personal experiences, especially when it comes to mindset, there are other ways to share. We will explore some of those going forward. The main resolution, though, could be to enhance the lives of others.

You can use your newfound confidence in your daily life. You can help yourself find more satisfying solutions that solve your inner child's need for art. You can fill your life with new exposures to art that seemed out of reach before releasing your instincts.

You can make a better world generally because you enjoy art now. We will talk about how later. Hand this book to someone whom you think has become inhibited about their own art life. Bring art into the workplace and surprise your coworkers. A new hat, a picture behind your desk, a colorful clipboard—it doesn't matter. Remember, we are not calling everything art; we are just noticing when it really is, and then we smile inwardly.

Help children. You probably know a child. Use the chance, if you can, to prevent some of the damaging events that will inhibit them later on. You know this to be true now, and you can help with a few well-chosen words.

Spread the word that art is not only for the rich, elite, educated, and knowledgeable. Be bold and tell folks you know better. You know what you like, and you go forward on that basis fully confident; it is all you need to know about art.

ART'S PLACE IN SOCIETY

The world often sees art as a frivolous endeavor. Early on, budding artists are warned, "You cannot make a living at this!" It is seen as a lazy, sort of slacker way of living. I guess the world thinks that unless it is painful, it cannot be taken seriously. Think of the "no pain, no gain" mantra about exercising. Actually, the opposite may be true. If one aligns with one's strengths, which inherently makes things fun and easy for that person to pursue the endeavor, it is often seen as silly or meaningless.

Dreamers are considered people who can't do but only dream. That also is not true. First, the dream. Then the effort. Then the success! Many dreams come true that way. Hard work is not the only path to success.

I do know that if one pursues what one is good at, one has a better chance at success. Success breeds success. The more successful our efforts are, the more we try, and the more we create the opportunity for full-blown success beyond our dreams. It's absolutely possible, and, for me, a much more sensible approach to success than driving hard in a drudgingly boring way on a path that never led to success in the first place.

It has been pointed out that when, in this culture, we see that a child is good at something, we often take them in the opposite direction. "Oh, you are good at reading? Well then, let's work on math!" I have to wonder why. That child will always be better at reading and will most probably be a successful reader, so why not go with his strengths? We can assume his weaknesses will always be weaker with less chance of success. I'll bet we could survey the population and find that successful careers are built on innate strengths, not weaknesses. When it comes to success, freedom is the answer.

There are many outreach opportunities to help promote art. Can you think of an activity that is going on right now in your world? A boys or girls club? After-school care?

Do you see yourself becoming a board member and advising others to be art aware?

Is there a place to volunteer? How hard would it be to give a couple of hours to a street fair? A stage production? A summer camp? A club? Sunday school? Holiday events?

There are art makers and art supporters. The two go hand in hand. Remember that art is about communication—senders and receivers. There is a place for you to support art if you want.

All of humanity thrives when more arts are present. I am now speaking of all the arts because when you go to your niece's ballet recital, it may not be the dancing that speaks loudly but the costumes and stage set. Art shows often have music. It is almost impossible to sort out one form of art as the only form you can enjoy. We are more capable than that. Our interests are more diverse than that. Isn't that a wonderful thought? Let art in. Open the door. And help others through as you, yourself, go through it.

We've said over and over that society needs art because it enriches everyone. It's a dull life without color. It's a dull life without choice. It's a terrible life without any freedom. It's a hard life to not feel confident. These are the gifts of learning to trust your art instincts and filling your life with art. It's well documented that societies that restrict artists and art making suffer in other ways—think Chairman Mao. Life becomes grim.

Now, think about that when you hear about budget cuts for local art programs or the discussion that arts and crafts are not important. Or that recess is a waste of time that could be used for studying. Be aware.

Your awareness now could be telling you that art needs a chance to exist alongside the other programs considered essential to a high-achieving society. Political influences can remove funding with the stroke of a gavel. School boards, community programs, and organizations for every age and society are all looking at art programs and their usefulness. Perhaps this discussion brings to life the importance of the community in our human experience and, therefore, our happiness. It takes a village! You now have a way to help.

BE AN ART ENCOURAGER

There is a famous Zen koan that says a student asked Nakaga-wa-Soen during a meditation retreat, "I am very discouraged. What should I do?" Soen Roshi replied, "Encourage others." You may be wondering, what does that look like? I will tell you this. Encouragement is more than cheerleading. It is protecting the *intention* of the effort. If a parent turns a drawing 'round and round,' the child knows immediately that the drawing failed to deliver the message. Obviously, the parent doesn't even know which way is up! Seeing that the parent didn't "get it" when looking at the drawing, the child immediately knows the drawing has failed. Instead of a possibly misunderstood gesture or word, how hard is it for you to always say, "GREAT! Good job. It's great." If you really can't tell what it is, say, "Can you tell me a story about this?" Children will be happy to tell you all about it as they are proud of it, and you are interested!

That reminds me of Johnny. Johnny drew a nativity scene for Christmas with Mary, Joseph, the baby Jesus, and a fat kid in the corner! The teacher said, "Johnny, tell me a story about this." Johnny said, "Well, that is Mary, and that is Joseph, and that's the baby Jesus." The teacher said, "And who is that in the corner?" "Oh," said Johnny, "that's Round John Virgin!"

See how delightful kids are? That is what we are trying to protect. Which voice do you want to contribute to those around you? Always provide a free and creative environment for you and for all the children around you.

ART INFLUENCERS: WHO ARE THEY? IS IT YOU?

Influencers exist in all of our lives. Even as adults, we seek out mentors, good counsel, compassionate friends, colleagues, and acquaintances. We take a class. We seek out someone we regard as a center of influence. In other words, someone who knows what they are talking about. You may be such an influence. Certainly, you influence those in your immediate circle, such as family. We are not talking here about what kind of influence, just that you do have influence.

The influence on children is of prime importance to this discussion as we know that those who influenced us as children caused either positive or negative growth in us. You then have an opportunity if you are around children in any sort of influencing position.

List some areas of your life where you encounter and, therefore, influence children.

Is there an opportunity to cause some positive art growth in their young world? By introducing an art activity? By removing some rules? By simply loving them and all they do?

Would you grow as a result of helping them grow?

Is there a regular time when you are teaching children? Coaching? Religious events? Organized club activities?

Have you been aware before now that you might have an opportunity to help children feel free while encouraging them to learn good, responsible content?

Does it have to be one or the other? Why not both?

CHAPTER 23

BE AN EFFECTIVE ART INFLUENCER

ARE YOU AN INFLUENCER IN SOME CHILD'S LIFE, IMPOSING rules that really don't matter? Think about it. Of course, some rules are necessary, but which rules? Make a note.

Which rules are you using that serve no real purpose?

Do you have any examples of some rules that are just habits?

Can you think of silly rules that you were made to apply that turned out to be meaningless? I know someone who was not allowed to sit on the couch unless his feet remained touching the floor. Really? Why would that rule exist? What is the assumption about the child and his feet? Can you see the damage? It's hard to daydream when you have to worry about whether or not your feet are touching the floor.

Jot down your thoughts.

You have to be able to solve problems without rules and stimulate creativity. Rules are limiting. Limiting imaginative possibilities restricts problem-solving. Applying new ideas requires thinking through a problem first and removing all previous assumptions. If you remove the rules, the potential for an imaginative solution exists more easily. Being able to freewheel in your mind allows for potentially crazy ideas to formulate. They often work!

WE ARE ALWAYS TEACHING

Are you a teacher? You most likely are, whether it is a formal title or not. Parents are teachers. Neighbors are teachers. We are all teaching each other all the time. Art can enhance the teaching experience in so many ways. One just must plan for it.

You can use art when teaching anything to anyone in *any kind* of classroom. You, as an influencing adult, may have an opportunity to develop easy, small, baby-step ways to incorporate art projects into your group activities. Find simple things you can do that are easy, cheap, and require little prep or effort. Why? Teaching is less boring when accompanied by visual art notes. The material learned sticks better.

As I mentioned, the great Swiss psychologist Jean Piaget reminded us that in order to learn a new thing, one had to have a "peg" in one's mind to hang it on, or it wouldn't stick. You know this is true if you have ever been told something totally irrelevant to you, just useless information that I'll bet you can't repeat today. The picture or action of making visual art creates that peg onto which one can put the new information so that it *is* relevant. That is why teaching using visual art can make learning so much better. Try it.

Can you think of an instance right now where the concept you are trying to teach would work better if there was a visual image attached to it? What about "star" charts for when kids do things and do them well? The kid gets a star for doing something well. The idea is to see progress and perhaps earn rewards. The real reward is seeing stars on that chart, even if they just appear on the fridge.

Jot down your ideas.

By the way, you are not too old for stars for yourself! Any time you challenge yourself to any new activity, it is always good to build in a reward. If you decide to check out the mall to see art scenes there, give yourself a nice lunch to go with it. We are all still children inside, and we need "attaboys," especially from the one who counts the most: ourselves.

ART THERAPY

Like teaching, we are always in therapy of some kind. Women joke about retail therapy (shopping to feel better). Sometimes, it's the sports bar, sometimes a good girlfriend chat, or maybe a Japanese forest bathing event. It is a sign of good mental health to include therapeutic sessions to ease what can sometimes be a difficult life. I am not talking about drugs or alcohol but, rather, experiences that are self-healing. Making art, looking at art, or anything to do with art certainly qualifies as self-healing. The great thing is you can be in control of this kind of activity for yourself whenever you want.

Art therapists rely upon visual art creation all the time because it works. If they can get a troubled child to draw the feelings about an incident or the incident itself, it releases the emotion. It gives the event significance and gives the child a place to put reactions surrounding it. Once the drawing, which now has put the issue out in the open, is revealed to the therapist, the healing work can be done. It's a wonderful healing process. The exercises that have been developed by art therapists are wonderfully freeing and worth exploring. Remember, a picture is worth a thousand words.

AN EASY SUCCESSFUL PROJECT TO TRY

Here is an easy way to bring visual art to any topic: cut up magazines. You don't have to buy art supplies, make them work, or know what you are doing to have success with torn-up magazine pages. You don't even need a pair of scissors for each person. Scraps of color-printed paper shapes can be put together with some glue and imagination. You can usually find a public place that has extra magazines to throw away; keep on the lookout if your participants can't find any.

Flour and water make glue, in case you didn't remember—no need for glue sticks, school glue, or even tape. Papier-mâché is simply white flour and water mixed into a paste to hold paper together. It works! It does work better with a brush, but fingers will do it.

The subject matter for this project is best if it is simple and easily understood by everyone of every level and age. You can make the object of this exercise fit whatever learning you want to take place. If you want to have just a fun exercise to bond people together, create a friendship circle of some sort, have something to do at the club, or a get-acquainted fun activity among strangers, try creating a still life.

A still life is a fancy name for a picture of a bowl of fruit. Everyone knows what fruit looks like. A round, red, circular shape is an apple. If it's orange, it is an orange, right? Invite others to make fruit-like shapes from what they find. They are not looking for the perfect red color; anything with other images in it, combined with other red-like colors and textures, all make for interesting apples. Remember, the person who will view the art piece also knows what apples look like, so a "close enough" image will do. They will recognize it just fine. As viewers, we only need reminders for the image to succeed.

The fruit shapes only have to be approximate. We have no rules and no perfectionism at work in this task. Just rough shapes. Now, make a bowl. A bowl-like shape. Half a circle sitting on its round edge, right? Something to put the fruit on. Arrange the shapes, and voilà! It's a bowl of fruit! Pasted on a piece of cardboard, where the background is a nice shade of brown or filled in with more magazine colors and shapes, it becomes magical. So fun. Everyone succeeds. It is so whimsical as not to be taken too seriously, which is mostly the point of the exercise. We are all about fun. Art at its best is always fun for the art maker.

YOU ALREADY DO THIS ART PROJECT—WANNA BET?
Who doesn't love cookies? Buy or bake some cookies. You know, the kind of plain sugar cookie. You can even buy a tube of dough and slice them off if you don't want to start from scratch.

Remember, we are looking for fail-safe projects. Decorating cookies doesn't have to only be associated with the holidays. In fact, you can decorate pancakes at any breakfast time for fun. Cookies are easy because they are hard enough to accept the frosting or "paint" easily. If you are baking your own, you can vary the shapes. ANY shape. Think of it. Coordinate it with what you are teaching. Baseballs for the team, triangles for the tent campers—you get what I mean.

The concept of keeping the project simple and doable is still the aim. No complicated or difficult subject matter. Can it become complicated? Yes, though keeping the competition and expectations out of it is more in keeping with our goal of success for everyone. Simple shapes support the color, which is the main attraction with balloon shapes, for instance, a smiley face, a pumpkin, or a snowman. And, of course, you get to eat the results after the compliments and fun you give others when they see the results!

Speaking of baking . . . since you have the oven on already, and we have proven that you remember how to use it, try baking your own clay figures. There are ingenious commercial clays that can be baked to hardness in one's kitchen oven. This is not inexpensive (available online or at a craft supply house). Because of its cost, it is best for tiny little projects for one's desk or a little souvenir reminder of a shared experience, not for making a kitchen bowl. It is not food safe, but it makes for an easy home project.

Remember, you are not just an influencer for groups; your family counts. An easy after-school or after-church activity, these clay-baking sessions can be a great lazy summer day boredom reducer. Just thought you should know. They'll love you for it.

My mother never made a pie without giving us a piece of the dough to build one of our own. The woodshed, the garage, the backyard, the basement, and the kitchen are all spaces where you can build something. It can be a temporary something or a real thing to keep forever. Do it with whatever materials you can scrounge up.

Scrounging is a wonderful skill. Check out the trash, especially the recycle bin. Think to yourself, "What does this look like? What else could it be?" Maybe those jar lids are actually eyes and could go on that board over there. Oh, there's some twine. *Hair!* Or maybe I could nail these two things together. That old plastic bottle looks like Popeye's arm to me. Where is the rest of him? He needs a pipe. And a head.

Amaze your friends by making a little garden ornament out of found stuff and enjoy the product as well as the process. You may wind up making one for your friend too.

Remember when we talked about looking versus seeing? Start seeing possibility. That's when your eyes leave off, and your imagination takes over. Your mind's eye is as powerful as the world seen with your real eyes. Maybe more.
These projects are great fun. How long has it been since you just puttered around with some free time one afternoon?
Could you find time again? When?
Maybe even sooner?

There are other fun ways to find the art that is all around you every day. Life is a mosaic of color and texture. "Mosaic" is a wonderful word and concept. Mosaics are a metaphor for life—many events and experiences (tiles) combine to create the exquisite, one-of-a-kind masterpiece we call life.

Have you ever made one? It is often a child's craft project. I have mosaics given to me by children around me who made hot pad trivets, plates covered with small pieces of broken tiles. Making mosaics is a fun way to experiment with an easily obtained material, and usually, it is very successful and pleasing to the eye.

There is something about using one's hands to make something out of nothing. I am reminded again of the joy of watching my mother take a string of yarn and manipulate it to create a sweater. Another metaphor for life. Perhaps doodling is the same thing—lots of scribbles, out of which some meaning starts to show itself.

We are also learning here that art can bring profound thoughts to your world. It often spurs deep emotions that reveal special insights we are better off knowing. I guess we know them and just need the reminder of them. That is another of art's jobs as we include it in our lives. It enriches our thoughts about how we are living and how we want to live. Even if the art is a story or tale, something we see as fantasy, it may touch a part of us that profoundly needs the reassurance the image brings.

Break some tile with a hammer. That already feels interesting, right? Like breaking the rules, we can break tile because we have a purpose. Put some glue on a plate, the floor, or a piece of wood or metal, and stick those pieces on it. You can practice with the shapes if you want to, but often, the first response is the best response. When you choose the tile, try to find something that is interesting to you because of color or pattern. The randomness of breaking tile with a hammer presents shapes that are inherently interesting because they are not the same. This will challenge your imagination. Do you see a recognizable image—a horse's head? A flower? A leaf? A stem? Or can it just be a collection of ingredients, much like life? I think so.

Try this alone or as a group project. It makes a great bath-

room floor. You can grout it with colored grout available anywhere to change the result once again. Playing is the objective
here. It is gratifying to have made something. Sort of a generous
gift to yourself. Trusting yourself to decorate in this way reinforces your art instincts. All children love to make mosaics.

THE RULES OF ART (SPOILER ALERT: THERE AREN'T ANY!)

There are no rules in making art. Start noticing art all around
you. Once you agree that creativity is problem-solving and that
freedom is an essential component of problem-solving, you will
see the place that rules have in the making of art: none.
Are you allowing yourself the freedom to look objectively at art?
When?
Write down some examples here of when you are exposed to art:

Could you make more opportunities for art experiences?
Where in your town are art opportunities? Think about this,
and write them down.

Are you allowing the children around you to just "be" with art? Are you sending signals that they are not acting properly somehow? Be careful! Note some areas here in which you might be cautious and aware of your actions and words. Art should always be a positive experience for everyone.

As we have repeatedly said, the conflict for the child is that their natural liking for art struggles to compete with their natural insecurity because they know they can't do things as well as adults can. It is so imperative to love them for being a child and doing a child's job at anything. Hang their artwork on the fridge and praise it to others within earshot of the kid.

Remember, there are no rules. Just love them and praise their process. By the way, don't make suggestions: you are an adult, but they don't need your instruction, just encouragement. And *don't draw it for them*! That only reinforces that they don't know how to do it well.

There is a simple way to encourage art if you are not in a place to directly influence through connection, talking, or participating. Write a check; we already talked about lack of funding. I was once told when I asked for $300 to buy a glass case to exhibit student works of art, "You're creative; figure it out!" All art programs everywhere could use a little more money. You will know it goes to a good cause. You may not see huge programmatic differences, but you may help club members, students, Sunday school kids, after-school programs, and art supply budgets in a significant way. Easy.

Can you think of a place for which to write a check? (A scholarship? An art club? Your local museum, even if it is not an art museum?)

ART'S WITHIN US—A NON-PROFIT

I have started a non-profit called Art's Within Us. Its mission is to create opportunities to influence others and bring more art awareness into the world. I hope to reach influencers who want to facilitate the exposition of the concepts I explain in this book to help children primarily and, of course, all art-insecure people everywhere. Not all people have the same access to art. They do since art is all around us if we perceive it as such, but often not in a formalized way. I would like to bring the notion that art is everywhere and easily accessible to more people. The extension programs will include library potentials, workshops, on-site and virtual trainings, and volunteer opportunities.

If you are interested in getting more information about how to take this book and its concepts into your community, please reach out. You may be able to help with the mission of discovering that Art's Within Us in a variety of ways.

I would love the chance to speak to you one-on-one about how you can contribute. You have talents and ideas that haven't become part of my program yet; we can collaborate. Remember, problem-solving is the crux of creativity and is most fun when it is a team sport. Let's buddy up and find others to help too. Just think of the lives we can touch and enrich.

I am planning on making P.A.T. online workshops available. What is P.A.T.? Who doesn't like a pat on the back? P.A.T. stands for Positive Art Training. Facilitators who want to expand their influence on others in their circle can learn how to push the boundaries of the concepts in this book to help others become more art aware and lead enhanced lives because of it. We may come up with even more ways for folks to recover their art instincts. Sounds like a good problem to solve.

Recently, I asked my little eight-year-old friend if she liked art. At eight years old, she is at a pivotal stage in her decision about whether or not art is for her. She said, *"Art is in my heart."* How gratifying to hear! That means her art instincts are still intact.

I hope your art instincts feel more intact now too. I hope you see how much art is always in your heart. I hope it remains there for all of your life. Let it go; let it grow. Trust your instincts. It's all about having fun.

CHAPTER 24

ART ADVENTURES

I FOLLOWED MY OWN INSTINCTS WHEN I DECIDED TO SHARE IN this book the notion that life is better when we trust ourselves. I feel honored you felt the same way—enough to stay with me and consider my suggestions. I hope you used the book as a diary and wrote down all your new art insights. Return to it yearly to see if it still sticks, and remind yourself about how much better life is with art in it.

I think you will find that you can't leave behind the concepts we have been discussing once they are embedded. If I did my job well, you can't go back. Once we see something new, we usually keep that as an integral part of the fabric of our being. That's the lovely thing about life: we keep growing. In this instance, I think art growth is positive growth, and I thank you for taking on the challenge.

I'm interested in what you thought, how you changed, and what might be included going forward. I am so interested in this topic and get such good reactions to it that I will pursue other avenues beyond this book. As you know, I am looking for those influencers who would like to join me in taking this to people who want it. I am not a revolutionary trying to change the world. I just want to enhance life a little with what I know is good and fun. The world could use more fun, eh?

Any progress you may have made on feeling good about art was always in you. If this book helped bring it out, I am grateful. I previously said that recovering your inner art voice was a form of self-love. I also believe that helping others through art is a form of love. Being an art encourager is a valiant intention. It can be done every day in small ways, as we have discussed. I am also interested in people who want to self-identify as an influencer. If you are such a person in your community, influencing any small group, family, or friends, or if you are a club organizer or teacher, I would love to help you further. Get in touch with me about your discoveries, questions, suggestions, and, of course, your victories. I also believe our instincts tell us that we have brilliance within us. Uncovering it is our lot in life. If you have brilliance to share with me, please do not hold back. Contact me.

Use this book as you go forward on your art awareness journey. Or start a new one. I have a new favorite journal from India, made from handcrafted leather with a jewel embedded in the cover. It is gorgeous. I feel special when I write in it. Let's remember, too, that writing is a way of touching your art spirit. Sometimes, it is just good to reflect. By talking to yourself on paper, you can sort out feelings—those emotions touched by something—and authenticate your reactions. This kind of processing is also valuable because it leaves a trail. You can document your feelings as you have done with this book, and you now have a diary of reactions to new concepts. I think recording the discomfort we feel when confronting a new way of thinking can help.

There is something about writing it down. We all know that goals written down are more often achieved. It somehow solidifies our thinking, and conclusions can be more obvious. Give yourself that advantage. Buy a book. If a special leather-crafted journal is intimidating, a spiral student notebook from the grocery store will do. Then write. Write down impressions. Give yourself an art journal for your continued art awareness journey.

This may be the final chapter of this book, but it is not the end, my friend. Let's stay in touch. It's not the end if you got caught by the art bug. It's a very infectious thing, and once bitten, you are never quite the same again. It is as if you have seen the other side. Once your imagination starts to dream again, it is just irresistible.

My guess is that you are different now. If you took my suggestions seriously, you cannot be the same. Small changes don't always feel profound, but over time, they grow and multiply. More attention to art means more satisfying experiences, more growth, and the yearning to do more and more of it. We are drawn to what feels good. That was the premise of this book anyway—that art is fun. You deserve more fun. As I have repeatedly said, you deserve more art in your life.

Now that your imagination faucet is turned on, ideas will begin to flow. You will see more than you did even a month ago. Remember I said you are not the same person you used to be? Well, that is a weekly, if not daily, statement if you continue to challenge yourself. Growth is always a good thing. Encourage others to expand with you. Be a leader, take someone to coffee, and talk about yourself and your new ideas about art. They may get the art bug too.

Enjoy. Art's within you.
LSY

Additional Related Reading

Bayles, David and Orland, Ted, *Art and Fear: Observations on the Perils (and Rewards) of Artmaking*, Capra Press Edition, Twelve Printings 1994–2000.

Bettelheim, Bruno, *The Uses of Enchantment*, Random House, New York, 1975.

Bloch, Douglas, with Jon Merritt, *Positive Self-Talk for Children: Teaching Self-Esteem Through Affirmations*, Bantam Books, New York, 1993.

Cameron, Julia, *The Artist Way: a Spiritual Path to Higher Creativity*, G. P. Putnam's Sons, New York, 1992.

Clifton, Donald and Nelson, Paula, *Soar with Your Strengths*, Dell Publishing, New York, 1992.

Dutton, Denis, *The Art Instinct: Beauty, Pleasure, and Human Evolution*, Bloomsbury Press, New York, 2009.

Faber, Adele and Mazlish, Elaine, *How to Talk So Kids Will Listen & Listen So Kids Will Talk*, Avon Books, New York, 1980.

Gilbert, Elizabeth, *Big Magic: Creative Living Beyond Fear*, Riverhead Books, New York, 2015.

Gray, Peter, *Free to Learn: Why Unleashing the Instinct to Play Will Make Our Children Happier, More Self-Reliant, and Better Students for Life*, Basic Books Publishing, New York, 2013.

Lowenfeld, Viktor and Brittain, W. Lambert, *Creative and Mental Growth*, The Macmillan Company, New York, 1970.

Nordby, Jacob, *The Creative Cure, How Finding and Freeing Your Inner Artist Can Heal Your Life,* Hierophant Publishing, San Antonio, TX 2021.

Robinson, PhD, Sir Ken, *Out of Our Minds: The Power of Being Creative*, John Wiley & Sons, Ltd., (UK) First Edition, 2001.

Robinson, Ken, and Aronica, Lou, *Creative Schools: The Grassroots Revolution That's Transforming Education*, Viking Penguin, a member of Penguin Group LLC (USA), 2015.

Stanier, Michael Bungay, *How to Begin*, distributed in the US by Macmillan, New York, 2022.

Wadsworth, Barry J., *Piaget's Theory of Cognitive Development: An Introduction for Students of Psychology and Education*, David McKay Company, Inc., New York, 1971.

Wasserman, Edward A., *As If by Design: How Creative Behaviors Really Evolve*, Cambridge, UK, Cambridge University Press, 2021.

Keep in touch as you expand your art journey. I want to hear all about your progress toward the joy of having more art in your life. Thank you for reading my book.

Louise Seirmarco-Yale

703.622.7972 hello@peopleneedart.com

Join the mission at her non-profit organization:
ArtsWithinUs.org support@artswithinus.org

Acknowledgments

You know how all authors say they cannot thank people enough or cannot thank enough people? Well, it's true.

How can I thank all those who taught me, helped me, comforted me, and encouraged me? How much gratitude is enough for those who guided me and those whose friendship helped me, and kept me whole, in my process of becoming?

I thank, again, my family, who always thought I could be more. Of course I dedicated this book to them as they dedicated their lives and support to me. Thank you, dear ones. Eternally.

Keeping me strong were two dear friends who ran with me every day for fifteen years and then had breakfast with me once a week for another thirty years. Thank you, Penny Blake and Nancy Thibadeau. To Greg Morris, who later helped me stay physically strong so that eighty feels like fifty. I am eternally grateful for my enormously good health. And those who helped me be my best.

I have to recognize John DeMartelli who taught me about real drawing. I was very lucky to have known this masterful artist. My life has been strewn with fortuitous encounters. Knowing him was exceptional good luck.

All I can say is that I am grateful to have encountered so many wonderful professionals, family, and innocent bystanders. I have had amazing teaching positions that allowed me to influence in the world of art. Those chances were given generously to me, thus enriching me.

I must thank all my art patrons who loved my work, collected it, and supported me as an artist. I was given phenomenal opportunities that afforded my imagination abundant ammunition to make art . . . forever. It is my life's work. I appreciate all those who came to shows and then brought their Bridge Club to the show! Thank you.

One cannot know everything. I need advice. I am grateful to my coaches who reliably and consistently guide me toward success: James Lawson and Angela Inzerillo at Impact Biz LLC. You know how I feel about you.

My brilliant son, Derek Yale, is a consistent inspiration, and often has the best advice, as he knows me so well. I rely on him for his expert knowledge, as well as my husband, Wendel, who has astute observations about what is practical and effective. They both encourage and protect me and help me navigate life. I am happy and grateful to have them.

My thanks to Ashley Mansour and her capable team at Brands Through Books, without whom this book would not exist. It might have been a pipedream or a pamphlet, but not a real, meaningful book. Words cannot express my good fortune in having you in my life. Thank you. A special word of thanks to Shelly Zevlever, who managed my book project with sensitivity and thorough guidance. I thank you. Couldn't have done it without you.

I would like to offer a special thank you to a special guy. My admiration and gratitude to Paul Neuviale, who, as my editor, provided astute insights that kept my book on track. As a creative person, it is hard to hold me back from my tendency to expand a thought. His firm hand on my message kept me true to my mission. He supported the message fully, and I am grateful.

I am most thankful to get this important message to the world of those who want to recover their childhood love of art. I wish them a wonderful art journey. It's worth it.

LSY

Joy through art to you all.

About the Author

Louise Seirmarco-Yale has been an artist, teacher, and influencer in the visual arts for more than six decades.

With a Bachelor of Fine Arts in Studio Art and a minor in teaching, her background eventually included teaching every level of student the various art techniques, as well as art theory, art criticism, and art appreciation.

After getting a Master of Fine Arts in Art History with a minor in higher education, Seirmarco-Yale went on to teach in a community college, teaching design and the history of the world's art. That background led her to the administration of the Docent Program at the Toledo Museum of Art.

Over a period of ten years, thirty years ago, the author sold over a thousand paintings from her studio in Reston, VA. Themed exhibits every six months led her to a local, national, and international reputation. Her painting studio remains active today as good painting ideas never stop. When Picasso was asked which was his favorite painting, he is said to have replied "the next one!" That is how Louise feels about being an artist. It is not like a garden where you can think, "I guess I won't put one in this year!" It is a lifetime commitment she made many years ago. Her inventory at this writing is well into the 3000s with more on the way.

The enormous engagement of the public in Louise's lectures has led to her observations about how the public views art. It became obvious that readers needed permission to trust their own judgment. Thus, the book *Art, You Be the Judge*. The book contains down-to-earth practical exercises to restore

the reader's confidence when it comes to art. These time-test-
ed, well-worn, belief-changing, thought-play exercises can
transform the reader's view of their own ability to make and
consume art again. The objective is to return to the joy art can
bring to daily life, enriching ordinary people and society.